Collins

AQA GCSE 9-1
Maths
Foundation

Trevor Senior, Anne Stothers and Leisa Bovey

Exam Skills
and **Practice**

How to use this book

This Exam Skills and Practice book puts the spotlight on the different types of command word – the instructional word or phrase in a question – you can expect to find in your GCSE papers. Each section has worked examples and lots of timed practice to help build your exam technique.

Top Tips offer nuggets of information to keep in mind when answering each type of question.

Scan the **QR code** to test your understanding of the command word and see worked solutions to the example question(s) on that page.

Each question shows the part of the specification and grade range you are working at. These icons show whether a calculator is allowed 🖩 or not 🚫.

Complete the example to take the next step in your practice. Parts of the workings and/or answers are given for you to finish. Helpful hints also steer you in the right direction.

Each **command word** is defined in easy-to-understand language.

Example questions show the command words in context. Use the QR code to access worked video solutions and commentary for them.

Exam practice questions enable you to delve deeper into each command word across a range of topics and grade levels. There is a target time for doing these at exam speed.

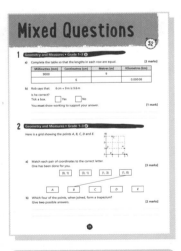

Mixed questions help to refine your exam skills with practice that recaps a variety of the command words.

An **index of topics** enables you to quickly find questions within the book from particular parts of the AQA GCSE specification.

Answers are given at the back of the book so that you can check and mark your own work.

Contents

Revise by command word!

Write (down)

Write: You may need to do some working to answer the question.

Write down: You should be able to answer the question without written workings.

Worked examples and more!

TOP TIP
You can quickly check your answers to these questions if you have time.

Example questions

1 Number • Grade 1–3

Write $\frac{17}{5}$ as a mixed number. [1 mark]

2 Algebra • Grade 3–5

Write down the integers satisfied by $2 < x \leqslant 6$ [2 marks]

Complete the example

Line *AB* is shown on the grid.

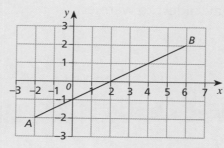

Write down the coordinates of the midpoint of *AB*.

[1 mark]

A has coordinates (−2, −2)

B has coordinates (6, 2)

From *A* to *B* is 8 across and 4 up, so halfway

from *A* to *B* is .... across and .... up.

So the midpoint of *AB* has coordinates

(.............. , ...).

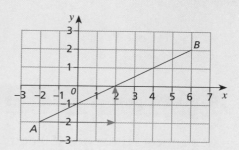

Exam practice questions

1

Geometry and Measures • Grade 1–3

Write down a suitable metric unit for each of the following.

[3 marks]

	Metric unit
Length of a classroom	
Mass of a person	
Amount of water in a large bottle	

2

Probability • Grade 1–3

An ordinary, fair six-sided dice is rolled.

Write down the probability it lands on 5

[1 mark]

3 Number • Grade 1–3

Here are four temperatures.

0 °C   −2.1 °C   0.5 °C   −3.5 °C

Write the temperatures from coldest to warmest.

[1 mark]

....

4 Geometry and Measures • Grade 1–3

Write down the size of angle x.

[1 mark]

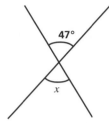

47°

x

$x =$ .... degrees

5 Ratio, Proportion and Rates of Change • Grade 1–3

At a concert there are 450 adults and 150 children.

Write the ratio of adults to children in the form $n : 1$

[2 marks]

....

6 Algebra • Grade 1–3

Here is a sequence of numbers.

34   28   22   16

a) Write down the next **two** numbers in the sequence.

[2 marks]

.... and ....

b) Write down the rule for continuing the sequence.

[1 mark]

....

7 Number • Grade 3–5

Write $(2^6 \times 2^4) \div 2^3$ as a single power of 2

[2 marks]

....

8 **Statistics / Probability • Grade 3–5** 🖩

22 students were asked to state the number of books they read in the last month.
The chart shows the replies.

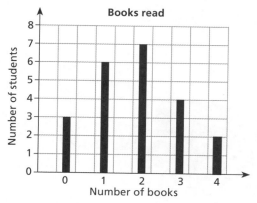

a) Write down the modal number of books. [1 mark]

b) One of the students is chosen at random.

Write down the probability that the student replied 0 books. [1 mark]

9 **Algebra • Grade 3–5** 🖩

a) Write a number in the box to make the calculation correct. [1 mark]

$17.5 - \boxed{} = 12.6$

b) Write a fraction in the box to make the calculation correct. [1 mark]

$15 \times \boxed{} = 5$

c) Write an expression in the box to make the statement correct. [2 marks]

$ab \times \boxed{} = 5ab^3$

10 **Algebra • Grade 3–5** 🖩

Here is a number pattern.

Line 1 $5^2 + 6 \times 5 = 5 \times 11$
Line 2 $4^2 + 6 \times 4 = 4 \times 10$
Line 3 $3^2 + 6 \times 3 = 3 \times 9$

Write down line 4 of the pattern. [2 marks]

Total score: _____ / 21

Which/What/When

These are similar to 'work out' and 'write down' questions but asked in a more direct way.

Worked examples and more!

TOP TIP
Make sure you show your working.

Example questions

1 Number • Grade 1–3 🖩

The sum of a square number and a cube number is 76

What are the **two** numbers? [3 marks]

2 Statistics • Grade 3–5 🖩

The table summarises the scores given in a quiz.

Score	1–5	6–10	11–15	16–20	21–25
Frequency	0	3	6	7	4

What is the modal class? [1 mark]

Complete the example

On the grid are seven triangles.

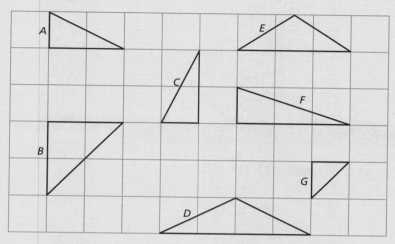

a) Which **two** triangles are congruent?   [1 mark]

Congruent shapes have exactly the same shape and size. They can be

rotations or reflections of each other.

.... and .... are congruent.

b) Which **two** triangles are similar?   [1 mark]

Similar shapes are enlargements of each other.

.... and .... are similar.

Exam practice questions

1

A purse contains 78p
Each coin has a different value.

What coins are in the purse?   [1 mark]

2 Ratio, Proportion and Rates of Change • Grade 1–3 🖩

On a model of a giraffe, 1 cm represents 0.5 metres.
The height of the model is 11 cm

What is the height of the giraffe?

[2 marks]

.... m

3 Number • Grade 1–3 🖩

a) What is 0.25 as a percentage?

[1 mark]

....

b) What is $\frac{3}{5}$ as a decimal?

[1 mark]

....

c) What is 65% as a fraction in its simplest form?

[2 marks]

....

4 Geometry and Measures • Grade 1–3 🖩

I am describing a quadrilateral.

When I draw in one of the diagonals, it makes two congruent triangles.
When I draw in the other diagonal, it makes two different isosceles triangles.

What is the name of the quadrilateral that I am describing?

[2 marks]

....

5   Number / Algebra • Grade 1–3

Here are the first eight terms of a sequence.

4, 7, 10, 13, 16, 19, 22, 25

a)   What type of sequence is it?

[1 mark]

....

b)   Which of these eight numbers are prime?

[2 marks]

....

6   Algebra • Grade 1–3

This sequence of patterns is made from rectangular tiles.

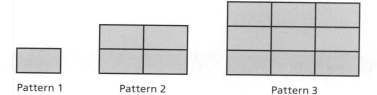

Pattern 1   Pattern 2   Pattern 3

a)   Which pattern uses 144 tiles?

[1 mark]

....

b)   Which pattern uses exactly the same number of tiles as Pattern 3
     and Pattern 4 combined?

[2 marks]

....

7   Number • Grade 3–5

A bell chimes every 15 minutes.
A light flashes every 8 minutes.
The bell chimes and the light flashes at 12 o'clock.

When is the next time the bell chimes and the light flashes at the same time?

[2 marks]

....

Ratio, Proportion and Rates of Change • Grade 3–5

Kitchen rolls come in packs of 2, 4 and 6 as shown.

£2.95   £5.40   £6.99

Which pack is best value?
You **must** show your working.

[4 marks]

Statistics • Grade 3–5

The graph shows the daily sales of a market trader.

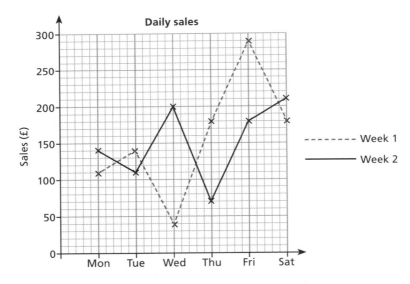

a)   Which day had the lowest total sales over the two weeks?   [2 marks]

b)   Which day had the greatest difference in sales over the two weeks?   [2 marks]

10 Probability • Grade 3–5

Here are eight cards.

| 1 | 2 | 3 | 4 | 5 | 6 | 7 | 8 |

Two cards are removed.
A card is then chosen from the remaining six cards.

The probability that the card chosen is prime is $\frac{1}{3}$

The probability that the card chosen is a factor of 6 is $\frac{2}{3}$

Which cards were removed?
You **must** show your working.

[3 marks]

.... and ....

11 Geometry and Measures • Grade 3–5

The diagram shows five straight lines.

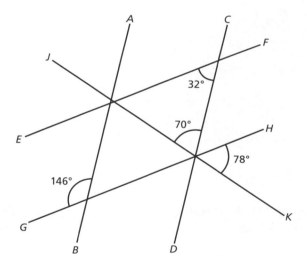

Which two lines are parallel?
You **must** show your working.

[2 marks]

.... and ....

Total score: .... / 30

How... long/ many/much/ does

Worked examples and more!

How long
How many
How much: Give a counted, measured or calculated answer.

How does this affect: Make a comment or a comparison to state how the answer changes in a given situation.

TOP TIP
You may need to do more than one step to answer the question.

Example questions

1 **Number • Grade 1–3** ▦

Billy is given £97 for his birthday.
He spends £29.99 on a game and £4.68 on lunch.
He saves the rest.

How much does Billy save? [2 marks]

2 **Ratio, Proportion and Rates of Change • Grade 3–5** ▦

A water tank is $\frac{1}{4}$ full.
20 litres of water are added to the tank.
It is now $\frac{7}{8}$ full.

How many **more** litres are needed to fill the tank? [3 marks]

Complete the example

Ana is putting small boxes into a large box.

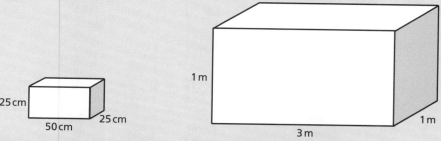

a)   How many small boxes can Ana fit into the large box?   **[3 marks]**

$3\,m$ = ... cm

To work out the number of small boxes that fit along the length, divide

.... cm by 50 cm. This gives .... small boxes across the length.

$1\,m$ = ... cm

To work out the number of small boxes that fit to the height and the

width of the large box, divide .... cm by 25 cm. This gives .... small

boxes in height and .... small boxes across the width.

The total number of small boxes that will fit inside the large box is

.... × .... × .... = ...

b)   The length of the large box is increased by more than 25 cm.

How does this affect the answer to part a)?   **[1 mark]**

Ana will be able to fit .... small boxes into the large box.

Exam practice questions

1

Parker works for 7 hours and is paid £66.50

How much is his hourly rate?   **[2 marks]**

£ ....

2 Statistics • Grade 1–3 🖩

The composite bar chart shows the numbers of teas and coffees sold in a café over 5 days.

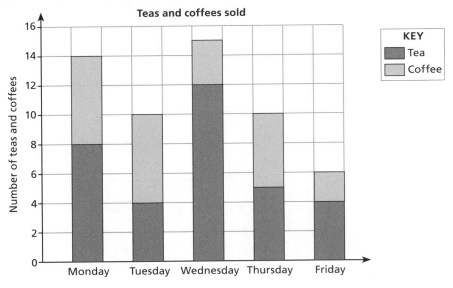

a) How many teas were sold on Thursday? **[1 mark]**

b) How many more teas than coffees were sold in total over the 5 days? **[2 marks]**

3 Number • Grade 1–3 🖩

Mo played 39 games of tennis.
He won $\frac{2}{3}$ of the games.

a) How many games did he win? **[1 mark]**

b) Mo played 3 more games and won them all.

How does this affect the fraction of games he has won? **[1 mark]**

4 Probability • Grade 1–3

A bag contains 60 counters.
They are red or blue.
The probability of choosing a red counter, at random, is 0.2

How many blue counters are in the bag?

[2 marks]

5 Ratio, Proportion and Rates of Change • Grade 1–3

A jug contains 1.2 litres of lemonade.
345 ml is poured into a glass.

How much lemonade is left in the jug?
State the units of your answer.

[3 marks]

6 Algebra • Grade 1–3

This sequence of patterns is made using small squares and circles.

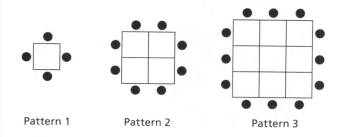

Pattern 1   Pattern 2   Pattern 3

a) How many circles are in Pattern 4?

[1 mark]

b) How many small squares are in Pattern 10?

[1 mark]

7 Ratio, Proportion and Rates of Change • Grade 3–5 🔢

Tom drives to meet a friend.
He drives a distance of 30 miles at an average of 40 mph.

a) How many minutes does his journey take?

[3 marks]

.... minutes

b) His speed on the way back was less than 40 mph.

How does the time on the way back compare with the time taken in part a)? [1 mark]

8 Geometry and Measures • Grade 3–5 🔢

A ladder is leaning against a wall as shown.
The foot of the ladder is 2.5 metres from the wall.
The top of the ladder reaches 8.75 metres up the wall.

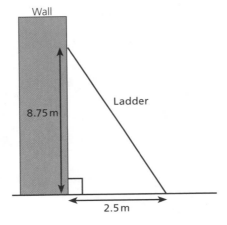

How long is the ladder?
Give your answer to 1 decimal place.

[3 marks]

.... m

9 Algebra • Grade 3–5

Three rods are placed together as shown in the diagram.
AB is 7 cm longer than AC.
BC is twice as long as AB.
The total length of the three rods is 73 cm.

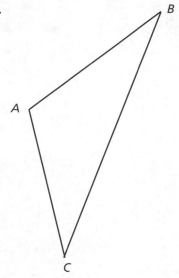

How long is AC?

[4 marks]

.... cm

10 Geometry and Measures • Grade 3–5

A cube has a total surface area of 96 cm²

How long is one edge of the cube?

[2 marks]

.... cm

11 Ratio, Proportion and Rates of Change • Grade 3–5

On a farm, the ratio of cows to sheep is 2 : 3
The ratio of cows to goats is 4 : 5
There are 36 sheep.

How many goats are there?

[3 marks]

....

Total score: .... / 30

Work out

Find the answer to a given problem.

Worked examples and more!

TOP TIP
You are likely to need to do one or more calculations.

Example questions

1 Number • Grade 1–3 🖩

Work out $3 \div 0.2$ [1 mark]

2 Geometry and Measures • Grade 3–5 🖩

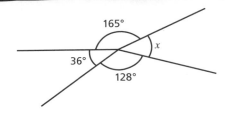

Work out the size of angle x.   [3 marks]

Complete the example

A car travels 4.5 kilometres in 10 minutes.

Work out the average speed in kilometres per hour.

[3 marks]

One hour = ... minutes

The car travels: 4.5 kilometres in 10 minutes

.... kilometres in 20 minutes

.... kilometres in 30 minutes

.... kilometres in 60 minutes

The average speed is .... km/h.

Exam practice questions

(35)

1 Number • Grade 1–3 ▦

Work out $4 + 7 \times 3$

[1 mark]

2 Number • Grade 1–3 ▦

Work out 57×26

[3 marks]

3 Statistics • Grade 1–3 ▦

Here is a list of numbers.

5   7   2   8   9   3

Work out the median value.

[2 marks]

4 Algebra • Grade 1–3

a) A square has a side length of x.
The perimeter of the square is 30 cm.

Work out the length x.

[2 marks]

$x =$ .... cm

b) Six squares with side length y are placed together to form a rectangle, as shown.

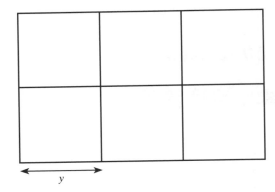

Work out an expression for the perimeter of the rectangle.

[1 mark]

....

5 Number • Grade 1–3

Samir buys 4 teas and 3 coffees.
The total cost is £12.30
One tea costs £1.65

Work out the cost of one coffee.

[3 marks]

£ ....

6 Number • Grade 1–3 🖩

Work out the value of $4^3 - \sqrt{121}$

[2 marks]

....

7 Algebra • Grade 3–5 🖩

Here is a linear sequence.

$$2, 9, 16, \ldots, \ldots$$

a) Work out the next **two** terms in the sequence.

[1 mark]

....

b) Work out the nth term of the sequence.

[2 marks]

....

8 Statistics • Grade 3–5 🖩

The table below shows the time, in minutes, taken by 20 students to complete a puzzle.

Time taken (t minutes)	Frequency		
$0 < t \leqslant 10$	1		
$10 < t \leqslant 20$	3		
$20 < t \leqslant 30$	4		
$30 < t \leqslant 40$	10		
$40 < t \leqslant 50$	2		

Work out an estimate for the mean time taken to solve the puzzle.

[3 marks]

.... minutes

Geometry and Measures • Grade 3–5 🖩

Work out $\quad 2\begin{pmatrix} -5 \\ 3 \end{pmatrix} - \begin{pmatrix} 2 \\ -2 \end{pmatrix}$

[2 marks]

$\begin{pmatrix} \quad \\ \quad \end{pmatrix}$

10 **Geometry and Measures • Grade 3–5** 🖩

The diagram shows two similar triangles.

$XY = 7.5\,\text{cm}$
$YZ = 12\,\text{cm}$
$AB = 2.5\,\text{cm}$

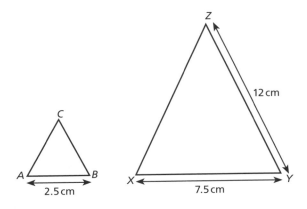

Work out the length of BC.

[2 marks]

$BC =$ .... cm

11 **Ratio, Proportion and Rates of Change • Grade 3–5** 🖩

The density of a piece of metal is 5.1 grams/cm³
The mass of the metal is 135.13 grams.

Work out the volume of the metal.

[2 marks]

.... cm³

12   Ratio, Proportion and Rates of Change • Grade 3–5 🖩

In an isosceles triangle ABC

angle A : angle $B = 1 : 2$

Work out **two** possible sizes of each angle.   **[4 marks]**

Angle A = ... degrees   Angle B = ... degrees   Angle C = ... degrees

Angle A = ... degrees   Angle B = ... degrees   Angle C = ... degrees

13   Number • Grade 3–5 🖩

Work out $(6.3 \times 10^9) \div (4.2 \times 10^6)$
Give your answer in standard form.   **[2 marks]**

....

14   Probability • Grade 3–5 🖩

In a game there are three possible outcomes, A, B and C.
$P(A) = 0.35$
$P(B) - P(C) = 0.15$

Work out $P(B)$ **[3 marks]**

....

Total score: .... **/ 35**

Calculate

These are similar to 'work out' questions but may be more difficult and you may need to use your calculator.

Worked examples and more!

TOP TIP
For most questions, working out will be required.

Example questions

1 Statistics • Grade 1–3 🖩

Here are the ages of 12 children at a party.

4   6   5   7   6   7   6   5   4   7   5   4

Calculate the mean age of the children. **[2 marks]**

2 Geometry and Measures • Grade 3–5 🖩

Calculate the area of a circle with radius 5.3 cm
Give your answer to 1 decimal place. **[2 marks]**

Complete the example

Here is a right-angled triangle.

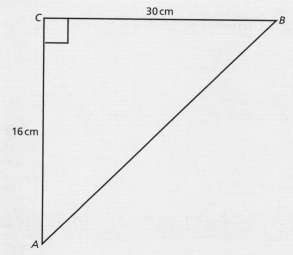

Calculate the length of *AB*.   **[2 marks]**

Pythagoras' theorem says that $a^2 +$ .... $=$ ....

Substituting in the numbers from the diagram gives ....$^2 +$ ....$^2 = AB^2$

This gives $AB^2 =$ .... and so $AB = \sqrt{\text{............}} =$ ....

The length of AB is .... cm

Exam practice questions

1

Number • Grade 1–3 🔳

The cost of 3 kg of apples is £2.52
The cost of 2 kg of pears is 96p

Calculate the total cost of 8 kg of apples and $2\frac{1}{2}$ kg of pears.   **[3 marks]**

£ ....

2   Algebra • Grade 1–3 🖩

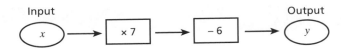

Input   Output

x → $\times 7$ → -6 → y

a)   Calculate the output y when the input is 1.5   **[1 mark]**

$y =$ ....

b)   Calculate the input x when the output is –30.15   **[2 marks]**

$x =$ ....

3   Number • Grade 1–3 🖩

A propeller rotates 2628 times in 6 minutes.

a)   Calculate the number of rotations per minute.   **[1 mark]**

....

b)   Calculate the number of rotations per second.   **[1 mark]**

....

4   Geometry and Measures • Grade 1–3 🖩

Here is a rectangle.

9.15 cm

7.26 cm

a)   Calculate the perimeter of the rectangle.   **[1 mark]**

.... cm

b)   Calculate the area of the rectangle.   **[1 mark]**

.... cm²

5 Number / Geometry and Measures • Grade 1–3 ▦

A map has a scale of 1 cm to 50 km.
The actual distance between Birmingham and Leeds is 210 km.

Calculate the distance, in centimetres, on the map between Birmingham and Leeds.   [2 marks]

.... cm

6 Geometry and Measures • Grade 1–3 ▦

In a quadrilateral, two of the angles are 73° and 89°.
The other two angles are equal.

Calculate the size of one of the other two angles.   [2 marks]

.... degrees

7 Ratio, Proportion and Rates of Change / Probability • Grade 3–5 ▦

A four-sided spinner is biased.

The table shows the probabilities that the spinner will land on B or on D.

Letter	A	B	C	D
Probability		0.25		0.15

The probability the spinner lands on A to the probability the spinner lands on C is 3 : 1

a) Calculate the probability that the spinner lands on C.   [3 marks]

....

b) Anya spins the spinner 80 times.

Calculate an estimate for the number of times the spinner will land on A.   [2 marks]

....

8 Geometry and Measures • Grade 3–5 ▦

A garden is in the shape of a square and a semicircle, as shown in the diagram.

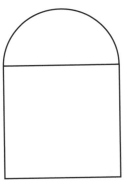

The radius of the semicircle is 3 m.
A bag of fertiliser covers 9 m² and costs £4 per bag.

Calculate the total cost of enough bags of fertiliser to cover the garden.   **[5 marks]**

£ ....

9 Ratio, Proportion and Rates of Change • Grade 3–5 ▦

Andi, Bao and Cara share some money.
Andi gets $\frac{3}{11}$ of the money.
Bao and Cara share the rest of the money in the ratio 2 : 3

Calculate the fraction of the total money that Cara gets.   **[3 marks]**

....

10 Number • Grade 3–5 ▦

a) Calculate $(56 - 13)^3$ **[1 mark]**

....

b) Calculate $\sqrt{1521} - 29$ **[1 mark]**

....

Number • Grade 3–5 🖩

Two different jars of coffee, A and B, are sold in a shop.

A   B

Calculate which jar offers the better value for money.
You **must** show your working.

[2 marks]

....

Number • Grade 3–5 🖩

a)   Calculate $3^5 + 6^3$

[1 mark]

....

b)   Calculate $\sqrt[3]{1331}$

[1 mark]

....

c)   Calculate   105% of £42

[1 mark]

£ ....

Total score: .... **/ 34**

Convert

Change a value from one numerical form to another, or a measure from one unit to another. You may need to use a calculation or read from a conversion graph.

Worked examples and more!

Example questions

1 Number • Grade 1–3 🖩

Convert   3700 millimetres   to metres.   [1 mark]

2 Ratio, Proportion and Rates of Change • Grade 3–5 🖩

16 ounces = 1 pound and 2.2 pounds = 1 kg

Convert   8 ounces   to grams.   [3 marks]

Complete the example

1 mile = 1.6 kilometres

Convert   1.5 kilometres per minute   to miles per hour.   **[2 marks]**

$1.5\,km/minute = 1.5 \,\rule{1cm}{0.4pt}\, 60\,km/h$

$\quad\quad\quad\quad\quad = 1.5 \,\rule{1cm}{0.4pt}\, 60 \,\rule{1cm}{0.4pt}\, 1.6\,mph$

So $1.5\,km/minute = \rule{3cm}{0.4pt} \,mph$

Exam practice questions

20

1   Number • Grade 1–3 ▦

a)   Convert   0.05   to a percentage.   **[1 mark]**

.... %

b)   Convert   0.05   to a fraction in its simplest form.   **[2 marks]**

....

2   Number • Grade 1–3 ▦

Convert $\frac{5}{16}$ to a decimal.   **[1 mark]**

....

3   Ratio, Proportion and Rates of Change • Grade 1–3 ▦

Convert   7 days   to minutes.   **[2 marks]**

.... minutes

4 Ratio, Proportion and Rates of Change • Grade 1–3 🔢

You are given that   1 fluid ounce = 28.4 millilitres

Convert   1562 millilitres   to fluid ounces.

[2 marks]

.... fl oz

5 Ratio, Proportion and Rates of Change • Grade 3–5 🔢

You are given that   £1 = 1.14 euros and £1 = 1.25 dollars

Convert   400 euros   to dollars.

[3 marks]

.... dollars

6 Ratio, Proportion and Rates of Change • Grade 3–5 🔢

A truck is travelling at 60 kilometres per hour.

Convert this speed to metres per second.

[2 marks]

.... m/s

7 Algebra • Grade 3–5 🔢

The formula for converting Celsius (C) to Fahrenheit (F) is

$$F = 1.8C + 32$$

Convert   15°C   to °F

[2 marks]

.... °F

8 **Ratio, Proportion and Rates of Change • Grade 3–5** 📱

Here is a conversion graph.

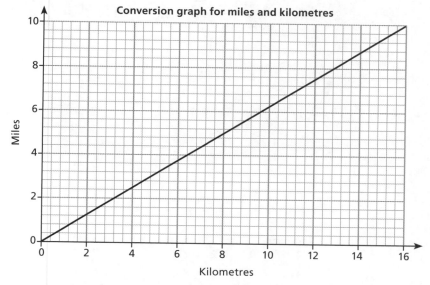

Conversion graph for miles and kilometres

Use the graph to answer the following questions.

a) Convert   8 miles   to kilometres.   **[1 mark]**

.... km

b) Convert   4 kilometres   to miles.   **[1 mark]**

.... miles

c) Convert   80 kilometres   to miles.   **[1 mark]**

.... miles

9 **Ratio, Proportion and Rates of Change • Grade 3–5** 📱

A recipe for bread uses 420 grams of flour.
1 cup holds 120 grams of flours.

Convert   420 grams   to cups.   **[2 marks]**

.... cups

Total score: .... / 20

Simplify (fully)

Collect terms or cancel a fraction to its lowest terms. This should always be done fully, even if the word 'fully' is not in the question.

Worked examples and more!

TOP TIP
The word 'fully' suggests more than one step is necessary.

Example questions

1 Algebra • Grade 1–3 🖩

Simplify fully $a + a + b - a + 2b + ab$ **[2 marks]**

2 Number • Grade 3–5 🖩

Simplify $(3\sqrt{5})^2$ **[2 marks]**

Complete the example

A bag contains red counters, blue counters and orange counters only.

There are $4x$ orange counters in the bag.

There are half as many blue counters as orange counters.

There are four times as many red counters as orange counters.

Write down the ratio of red counters to blue counters to orange counters.

Simplify your answer.

[2 marks]

Start this question by writing the number of orange counters as $4x$ and write expressions for the number of red and blue counters.

Red : Blue : Orange = ... : .... : $4x$

Red : Blue : Orange = ... : .... : 4

Now write the ratios as numbers only.

Red : Blue : Orange = ... : .... : ....

And finally, simplify your answer.

Exam practice questions

(25)

1

a) Simplify $d + 2d + 3d$

[1 mark]

b) Simplify $3a - 4b - 2a + 3b$

[2 marks]

c) Simplify $4cd - 8cd + 2cd$

[1 mark]

d) Simplify $2x^2 - 5x^2 + x^2$

[1 mark]

2   Algebra • Grade 1–3 🖩

a)   Simplify $2a \times 7$ **[1 mark]**

b)   Simplify $2b \times 9b$ **[1 mark]**

c)   Simplify $c \times 4 \times d \times 7$ **[1 mark]**

d)   Simplify $4e^2 \times 3e^3$ **[1 mark]**

3   Ratio, Proportion and Rates of Change • Grade 1–3 🖩

Simplify fully $275\,\text{mm} : 25\,\text{cm}$ **[2 marks]**

       :

4   Number • Grade 3–5 🖩

a)   Simplify $2^4 \times 2^7$ **[1 mark]**
       Write your answer as a power of 2

b)   Simplify $5^7 \div 5^{-1}$ **[1 mark]**
       Write your answer as a power of 5

5   Algebra • Grade 3–5 🖩

a)   Simplify fully $(2x^3)^4$ **[2 marks]**

b)   Simplify fully $\dfrac{8y^6}{2y^2}$ **[1 mark]**

6 Algebra / Statistics • Grade 3–5 🖩

Here are expressions for the heights of three students.

    Saya $(6x + 4)$ cm   Alex $(5x - 17)$ cm   Lily $(4x + 25)$ cm

Work out an expression for the mean of their heights.
Simplify your answer.

[2 marks]

.... cm

7 Algebra / Geometry and Measures • Grade 3–5 🖩

The lengths of the sides of a triangle are $(x + 3)$ cm, $(3x - 2)$ cm and $(5x - 4)$ cm

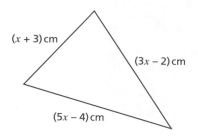

$(x + 3)$ cm

$(3x - 2)$ cm

$(5x - 4)$ cm

Work out an expression, in terms of x, for the perimeter of the triangle.
Simplify your answer.

[2 marks]

.... cm

8 Algebra / Geometry and Measures • Grade 3–5 🖩

The diagram shows a square inside a circle.

The square has side lengths of $2x$ cm.
The radius of the circle is y cm.

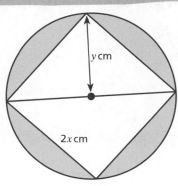

y cm

$2x$ cm

a)   Write down an expression for the area of the square.
     Simplify your answer.

[2 marks]

.... cm²

b)   Work out an expression for the shaded area.

[2 marks]

.... cm²

Total score: .... / 24

Multiply out/Expand

Worked examples and more!

Multiply out: Multiply out the brackets. In some questions, working out will be required and should be shown.

Expand: These are similar to 'multiply out' questions; you will usually need to simplify answers.

TOP TIP
Collect like terms where possible.

Example questions

1 Algebra • Grade 1–3 🖩

Multiply out and simplify $2(f + 9) + 3(f - 1)$ [2 marks]

2 Algebra • Grade 3–5 🖩

Expand and simplify $(x + 4)(x - 4)$ [2 marks]

Complete the example

Multiply out $(y + 3)(y + 5)$ **[2 marks]**

$(y + 3)(y + 5)$ means $(y + 3)$ multiplied by $(y + 5)$

Multiplying each term inside the first bracket by each term inside the second bracket:

$y \times y =$ ....   and $y \times 5 =$ ....

$3 \times$ .... $=$ ....   and $3 \times$ .... $=$ ....

Adding all the terms: .... + ... + ... + ...

Simplifying: ....

Exam practice questions

1   Algebra • Grade 1–3

a)   Multiply out $2(3x + 7)$ **[1 mark]**

....

b)   Multiply out and simplify $5x + 3(x - 3y)$ **[2 marks]**

....

2   Algebra • Grade 1–3

Multiply out $w(w^2 + 5)$ **[2 marks]**

....

41

3 Algebra • Grade 1–3

a) Multiply out $-2(4 - 3d)$ **[1 mark]**

b) Multiply out and simplify fully $6a - 3(a + 3)$ **[1 mark]**

4 Algebra • Grade 1–3

Multiply out and simplify fully $5(3a - 2) - (7a - 3)$ **[2 marks]**

5 Algebra • Grade 3–5

a) Multiply out and simplify $(p - 3)^2$ to show that $(p - 3)^2 \neq p^2 - 9$ **[2 marks]**

b) Multiply out $(2p - 3)^2$ **[2 marks]**

6 Algebra • Grade 3–5

Multiply out and simplify $(t + 3)^2 + (t - 4)^2$ **[3 marks]**

7 Algebra / Geometry and Measures • Grade 3–5

The diagram shows a rectangle.

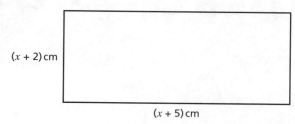

$(x + 2)$ cm

$(x + 5)$ cm

By expanding the brackets, show that the area of the rectangle is equal to $(x^2 + 7x + 10)$ cm²

[2 marks]

....

....

....

....

8 Algebra • Grade 3–5

a) Multiply out and simplify $(x + 5)(x - 2)$

[2 marks]

....

b) Multiply out and simplify $(5y - 3)(2y - 7)$

[2 marks]

....

9 Algebra • Grade 3–5

Multiply out and simplify $(x + 2)^2 - (x - 2)^2$

[3 marks]

....

Total score: .... / 25

Factorise (fully)

Take out any common factors or convert a quadratic expression into two linear factors. This should always be done fully, even if that word is not in the question.

Worked examples and more!

TOP TIP
The word 'fully' is a hint that more than one factor can be taken out.

Example questions

1 Algebra • Grade 1–3

Factorise $12x + 4$ [1 mark]

2 Algebra • Grade 3–5

Factorise $x^2 - 121$ [1 mark]

Complete the example

Factorise $x^2 + 6x + 5$ **[2 marks]**

This is a quadratic expression, as it is in the form $ax^2 + bx + c$, and it will factorise into two linear brackets.

The two numbers in the brackets will multiply to equal 5 and add to equal 6:

$(x +$ ....)$(x +$ ....$)$

Exam practice questions

(25)

1

Algebra • Grade 1–3

a) Factorise $3a - 15$ **[1 mark]**

b) Factorise fully $6a + 24b$ **[1 mark]**

c) Factorise fully $4a + 8b + 12c$ **[1 mark]**

d) Factorise $d^2 + d$ **[1 mark]**

e) Factorise $7e + 14e^2$ **[1 mark]**

2 Algebra • Grade 1–3

a) Factorise fully $16c^2 - 4c$ **[2 marks]**

....

b) Factorise fully $-10d^3 + 15d^2 + 5d$ **[2 marks]**

....

3 Algebra • Grade 1–3

Three students are given this question.

     Factorise fully $12x^2 + 8x$

These are their answers.

    $4(3x^2 + 2x)$ $2x(6x + 4)$ $4x(3x + 2)$

Which answer is correct?   **[1 mark]**

....

4 Algebra • Grade 3–5

a) Factorise fully $4ef^2 + 6e^2fg$ **[2 marks]**

....

b) Factorise fully $15x^3y - 6x^2y^3 + 21xy^2$ **[2 marks]**

....

5   Algebra • Grade 3–5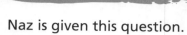

Naz is given this question.

    Factorise $x^2 - 7x + 12$

She writes, $x^2 - 7x + 12 = (x + 3)(x + 4)$ because $3 \times 4 = 12$

She is incorrect.

Write down the correct answer.   **[1 mark]**

6   Algebra • Grade 3–5

a)   Factorise $x^2 + 8x + 15$ **[2 marks]**

b)   Factorise $x^2 + 2x - 35$ **[2 marks]**

c)   Factorise $x^2 - 11x + 24$ **[2 marks]**

d)   Factorise $x^2 - 7x - 18$ **[2 marks]**

7   Algebra • Grade 3–5

a)   Factorise $x^2 - 9$ **[1 mark]**

b)   Factorise $x^2 - 121$ **[1 mark]**

Total score: / 25

Solve/Rearrange

Solve: Work out the value or values that satisfy a given equation or inequality.

Rearrange (... to make ... the subject): Write the given formula with a different subject as specified in the question.

Worked examples and more!

TOP TIP
Take a step-by-step approach to solving equations and rearranging formulae.

Example questions

1 Algebra • Grade 1–3 📱

Solve $\frac{x}{2} = 4$

[1 mark]

2 Algebra • Grade 3–5 📱

Rearrange $a = 3b + 7$ to make b the subject.

[2 marks]

Complete the example

Solve the simultaneous equations

$$a + 3b = 17$$
$$a + b = 7$$

You **must** show your working.
Do **not** use trial and improvement.

[2 marks]

Eliminate one variable. Do this by either adding or subtracting the equations. The coefficient of a is the same in both equations, so subtract the equations to eliminate the variable a.

Subtracting the equations to eliminate a:

.... + ... = ...

$a + b = 7$ —

.... = ...

And solving to find b: $b = $ ....

Substituting $b = $ .... into one of the original equations:

$$a + (3 \times 5) = 17$$
$$a + 15 = 17$$
$$a = \text{..............}$$

Finally, checking the answers by substituting into the other equation:

.... + 5 = ...

Exam practice questions

a) Solve $a - 8 = 13$

[1 mark]

$a = $ ....

b) Solve $\frac{b}{4} = 12$

[1 mark]

$b = $ ....

c) Solve $8c = 1$

[1 mark]

$c = $ ....

2 Algebra • Grade 1–3 🖩

Rearrange $y = 3x - 6$ to make x the subject.

[2 marks]

....

3 Algebra • Grade 1–3 🖩

a) Solve $8a + 10 = 66$

[2 marks]

$a = $ ....

b) Solve $6b - 12 = 2b + 20$

[2 marks]

$b = $ ....

c) Solve $3(c - 1) = 7c - 1$

[2 marks]

$c = $ ....

4 Algebra • Grade 3–5 🖩

A triangle has angles of
  $6x - 35°$
  $3x - 22°$
  $x + 12°$

Form and solve an equation to work out the size of x.

[3 marks]

$x = $ .... degrees

5 Algebra • Grade 3–5 🖩

Rearrange the formula to make x the subject.

$$y = \frac{x - 4}{3}$$

[2 marks]

....

50

6   Algebra • Grade 3–5

Solve the simultaneous equations
$$x + y = 3$$
$$3x - y = 11$$

You **must** show your working.

[3 marks]

$x =$ .... $y =$ ....

7   Algebra • Grade 3–5

Solve $3x - 8 < 13$

[2 marks]

....

8   Algebra • Grade 3–5

Solve the equation $x^2 + x - 12 = 0$

[3 marks]

$x =$ .... or $x =$ ....

9   Algebra • Grade 3–5

Use the graphs to solve the simultaneous equations $y = 3x + 1$
$$y + 2x = 11$$

[1 mark]

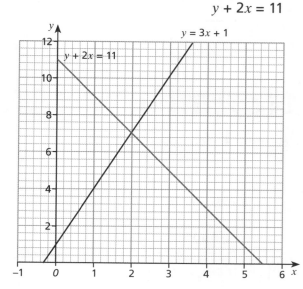

$x =$ .... $y =$ ....

Total score: .... / 25

Match

Worked examples and more!

Join corresponding items in two lists by lines.

TOP TIP
Only draw one line from each box on the left.

Example questions

1 Algebra • Grade 1–3 🖩

Match the algebra to the correct description.
One has been done for you.

[2 marks]

y	Formula
$A = \pi r^2$	Inequality
$3x < 8$	Equation
	Term

2 Ratio, Proportion and Rates of Change • Grade 3–5 🖩

Match each statement to its multiplier.

[4 marks]

	0.2
Increase by 20%	0.5
Double	0.8
Decrease by 80%	1.2
Halve	1.5
	2.0

Complete the example

Match each regular polygon to the size of its interior angle.
One has been done for you.

[3 marks]

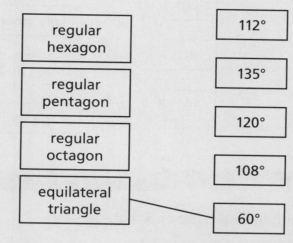

To calculate an interior angle of a regular polygon:

Step 1   Use   exterior angle = 360° ÷ number of sides

Step 2   Use   interior angle = 180° − exterior angle

A regular hexagon has 6 sides so

Step 1   Exterior angle = 360° ÷ 6 = ...°

Step 2   Interior angle = 180° − ....° = ...°

Exam practice questions

⏱ 20

1

Match each sequence to its description.
One has been done for you.

[2 marks]

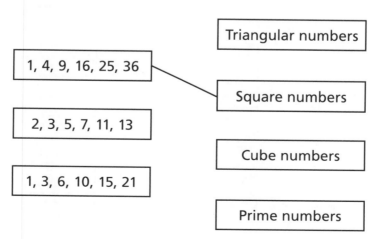

53

2 Geometry and Measures • Grade 1–3

Match each angle to its correct name.
One has been done for you.

[2 marks]

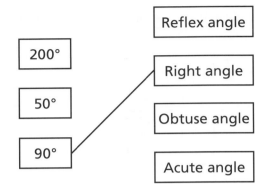

200°	Reflex angle
50°	Right angle
90°	Obtuse angle
	Acute angle

3 Number • Grade 1–3

Match each fraction with the equivalent percentage.
One has been done for you.

[4 marks]

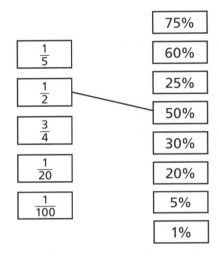

Left: $\frac{1}{5}$, $\frac{1}{2}$, $\frac{3}{4}$, $\frac{1}{20}$, $\frac{1}{100}$

Right: 75%, 60%, 25%, 50%, 30%, 20%, 5%, 1%

4 Ratio, Proportion and Rates of Change • Grade 3–5

Match each ratio on the left with the equivalent ratio on the right.
One has been done for you.

[3 marks]

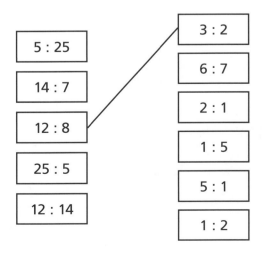

Left: 5 : 25, 14 : 7, 12 : 8, 25 : 5, 12 : 14

Right: 3 : 2, 6 : 7, 2 : 1, 1 : 5, 5 : 1, 1 : 2

5 Algebra • Grade 3–5

Match each expression or term on the left with the equivalent term on the right.
One has been done for you.

[3 marks]

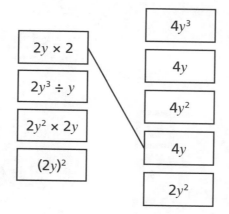

$2y \times 2$	$4y^3$
$2y^3 \div y$	$4y$
$2y^2 \times 2y$	$4y^2$
$(2y)^2$	$4y$
	$2y^2$

6 Number • Grade 3–5

Match the numbers written in standard form with their equivalent ordinary number.
One has been done for you.

[3 marks]

5.5×10^2	0.055
5.5×10^0	550
5.5×10^1	0.55
5.5×10^{-1}	55
	5.5

7 Algebra • Grade 3–5

Match the sequences on the left with their nth terms.
One has been done for you.

[3 marks]

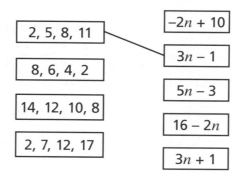

2, 5, 8, 11	$-2n + 10$
8, 6, 4, 2	$3n - 1$
14, 12, 10, 8	$5n - 3$
2, 7, 12, 17	$16 - 2n$
	$3n + 1$

Total score: _____ / 20

Complete/List

Complete: Add missing information to a table or diagram.

List: Write all possible answers.

Example question

1 Statistics • Grade 1–3

15 students are asked to choose an activity.

Their choices are

Climbing	Painting	Swimming	Sailing	Climbing
Climbing	Climbing	Painting	Sailing	Painting
Swimming	Swimming	Painting	Climbing	Climbing

Complete the tally and frequency columns in the table.   **[2 marks]**

Activity	Tally	Frequency
Climbing		
Painting		
Sailing		
Swimming		

Complete the example

Here are four number cards.

(1) (4) (8) (9)

List **all** the possible two-digit numbers that can be made using two of the cards.
The first three have been done for you.

14, 18, 19, ... **[2 marks]**

Writing down all the two-digit numbers starting with 1:

14, 18, 19

Then all the two-digit numbers starting with 4.

And so on.

14, 18, 19, 4...., ..., ..., 8...., ..., ..., 9...., ..., ...

Exam practice questions

1 Probability • Grade 1–3

A shop sells ribbons in four colours, blue (B), white (W), red (R) and pink (P).
Fay buys two ribbons.

List **all** the possible choices. **[2 marks]**

....

....

2 Statistics • Grade 1–3

A shop sells these 15 drinks in a 30-minute period.

Tea	Coffee	Coffee	Coffee	Juice
Coffee	Tea	Tea	Juice	Juice
Tea	Tea	Juice	Coffee	Tea

Complete the table. **[2 marks]**

Drink	Tally	Frequency
Tea		
Coffee		
Juice		
		Total = 15

3 Probability • Grade 1–3 🖩

Two ordinary six-sided dice are thrown.
The numbers the dice land on are added to give the score.

Complete the table below showing all the possible scores.   [2 marks]

First dice

		1	2	3	4	5	6
Second dice	1	2	3				
	2	3	4				
	3						
	4						
	5						
	6						

4 Number • Grade 1–3 🖩

List all the factors of 32   [2 marks]

....

....

5 Statistics • Grade 3–5 🖩

A netball team played 43 games.
23 games were played at home and the rest were played away.

The team won a total of 26 games.
They drew 11 games away.
1 of the 3 games they lost was at home.

Complete the table.   [3 marks]

	Won	Drawn	Lost	Total
Home			1	23
Away		11		
Total	26		3	43

6 Algebra • Grade 3–5 🖩

List the integers that satisfy both of these inequalities.

$2x - 5 > 0$ and $x < 10$

[2 marks]

....

....

7 Algebra • Grade 3–5 🖩

In a bag there are grey, black, orange and purple beads.

There are four more black beads than grey beads.

There are twice as many orange beads as black beads.

There are three fewer purple beads than orange beads.

Complete the table.

[3 marks]

Colour of bead	Number of beads
Grey	n
Black	
Orange	
Purple	

8 Ratio, Proportion and Rates of Change • Grade 3–5 🖩

Some women and men are asked if they are left-handed or right-handed.

There are 20 women.

There are three times as many men as women.

25% of the men are left-handed.

left-handed women : left-handed men = 2 : 5

Complete the two-way table.

[5 marks]

	Women	Men	Total
Left-handed			
Right-handed			
Total			

Total score: .... / 21

Estimate

Estimate a value from a graph: Read or interpret a value (it may be approximate) from a graph.

Estimate a probability: Use relative frequency to estimate a probability.

Estimate the value of a calculation: Round the numbers (usually to 1 significant figure) in a calculation to obtain an estimated answer.

Estimate a mean from a grouped frequency: Use the midpoints of the class intervals to calculate an approximate value of the mean.

Estimate a length: Use a scale drawing or map to estimate an actual distance.

Worked example and more!

TOP TIP
The symbol ≈ means 'approximately equal to'.

Example question

1 Number • Grade 1–3 📟

Use approximations to **estimate** the value of $\frac{28 \times 102}{64}$ **[2 marks]**

Complete the example

Here is the graph of $\quad y = x^2 - 8x + 19$

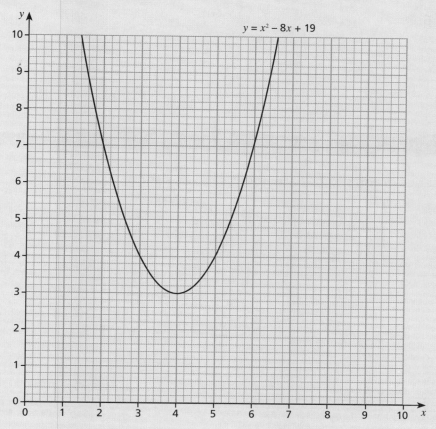

Use the graph to estimate the values of x when $y = 5$ **[3 marks]**

Use a ruler to draw a line from $y =$ .... to intersect with the curve.

Use a ruler to draw lines from the intersection of $y = 5$ and the curve to the

....

When $y = 5$, $x \approx 2.6$ and $x \approx$ ....

> When reading off from the graph, look carefully at the scale and make your estimate as accurate as possible.

Exam practice questions

1

By rounding each number to the nearest 10, estimate the value of $\quad \dfrac{8.1 \times 45.8}{18}$ **[2 marks]**

2 Probability • Grade 1–3 ▦

A dice is rolled 200 times.
It lands on the number 6 a total of 38 times.

Use relative frequency to estimate the probability that the next time the dice is rolled
it lands on 6
[1 mark]

....

3 Statistics • Grade 3–5 ▦

This time-series graph shows data about sales in a shop.

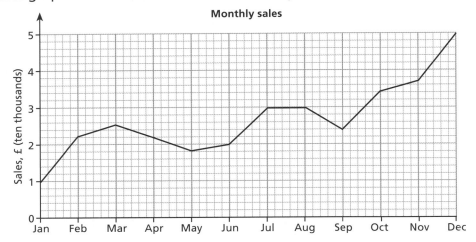

Estimate the sales in April.
[2 marks]

£ ....

4 Statistics • Grade 3–5 ▦

Here is some data about the time students take to travel to school.

Time (t minutes)	Frequency (f)	Midpoint	
$0 < t \leqslant 10$	15		
$10 < t \leqslant 20$	25		
$20 < t \leqslant 30$	10		
$30 < t \leqslant 40$	5		

Estimate the mean journey time to school.
Give your answer to 2 decimal places.
[3 marks]

.... minutes

5 Statistics • Grade 3–5

The scatter graph shows the estimated value of a car compared with its age.

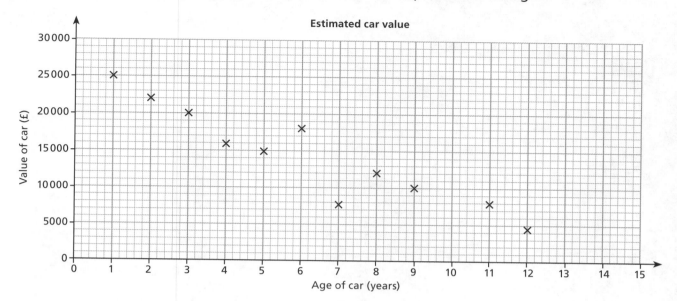

Use a line of best fit to estimate the value of the car when it is 10 years old.   **[3 marks]**

£ ....

6 Algebra • Grade 3–5

Here is a graph of $y = x^3$

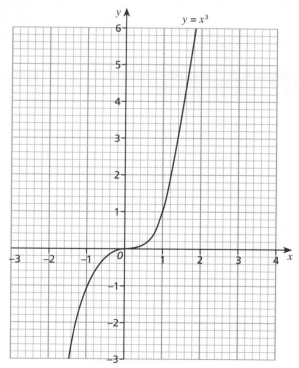

Use the graph to estimate the value of 1.5^3 **[2 marks]**

....

Total score: .... / 13

Draw/Sketch/Plot

Draw: Draw a graph or diagram accurately.

Sketch: Make an approximate drawing of a graph or diagram, showing the correct general shape with important points or distances labelled.

Plot: Mark points (with a cross) on a grid.

Worked example and more!

TOP TIP
Use a sharp pencil.

Example question

1 Algebra / Geometry and Measures • Grade 1–3

A, *B* and *C* are points on a coordinate grid.
A is the point (−2, −1)
B is the point (−1, 1)
C is the point (2, 1)

a) Plot points *A*, *B* and *C* on the grid. **[2 marks]**

b) *ABCD* is a trapezium.

D is a point on the line $x = 3$

Draw the trapezium on the grid. **[1 mark]**

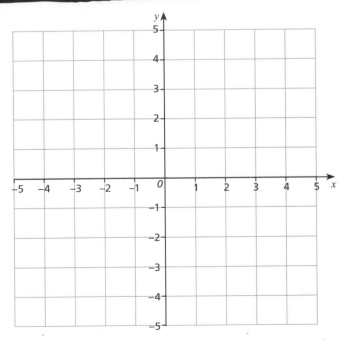

Complete the example

A teacher asked 120 students their favourite subject to study in science.

$\frac{1}{4}$ said Chemistry.

40% said Biology.

The remainder said Physics.

Draw and label a pie chart to show the data.   **[3 marks]**

The angles in a pie chart represent the proportion of each subject. There are 360° in a circle, so you need to find each proportion of 360°.

Chemistry: $\frac{1}{4}$ of ....° = ...°

Biology: 40% of 360° = (360 ÷ 10) × .... = ...°

Physics: 360° − (............................ + ...) = ...°

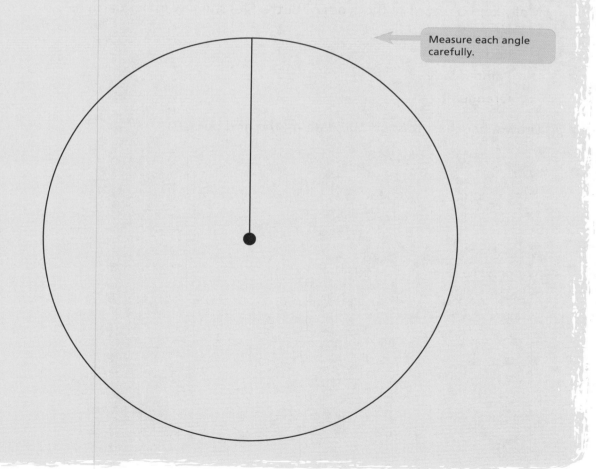

Measure each angle carefully.

Exam practice questions

1 Geometry and Measures • Grade 1–3

Here is a circle.

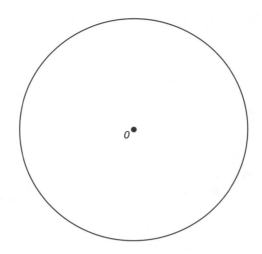

a)   Draw a diameter of the circle.   **[1 mark]**

b)   Draw a sector of the circle.   **[1 mark]**

2 Statistics • Grade 1–3

Molly kept a record of the types of butterflies she saw in her garden.

Peacock	4
Red admiral	6
Painted lady	5
Orange tip	2

Draw a bar chart to show the data on the grid below.   **[3 marks]**

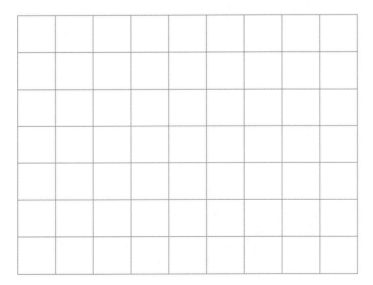

3 | Ratio, Proportion and Rates of Change • Grade 1–3 🖩

A rectangular field has a length of 80 m and a width of 50 m.

Draw the field on the grid below.
Use a scale of 10 m = 1 cm

[1 mark]

10 m = 1 cm

4 | Geometry and Measures • Grade 1–3 🖩

Sketch a net of this triangular prism.

[2 marks]

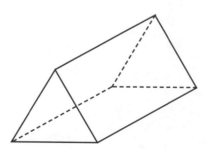

5 Algebra • Grade 3–5

On the grid, draw the graph of $y = 2x + 3$ from $x = -1$ to $x = 3$ **[3 marks]**

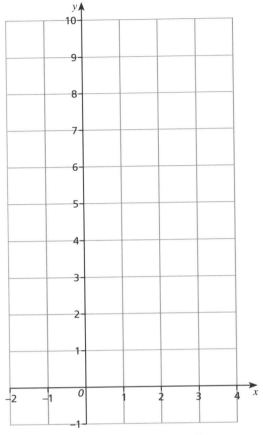

6 Geometry and Measures • Grade 3–5

Here is a 3D solid made of cubes.

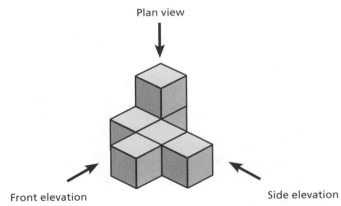

Plan view

Front elevation

Side elevation

On the grids, draw the plan view, front elevation and side elevation.   **[3 marks]**

Plan view   Front elevation   Side elevation

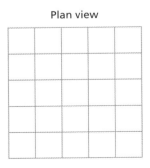 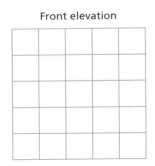 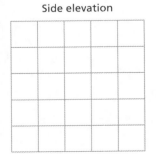

7 Statistics • Grade 3–5

The scatter graph shows the scores obtained by 10 students in two tests.

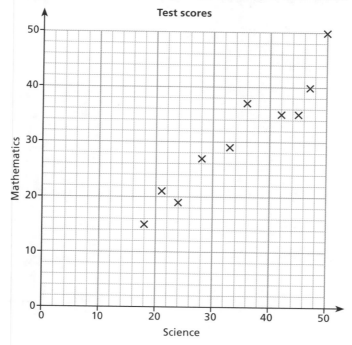

Draw a line of best fit on the grid.

Use your line of best fit to estimate the mathematics score for a student who has a score of 38 in science.

[2 marks]

....

8 Algebra • Grade 3–5

Sketch the graph of $y = x^2 + 3$

[2 marks]

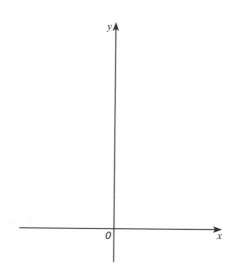

Total score: .... **/ 18**

Is ... correct?

Decide if a statement is correct and provide a reason. You **must** show working or give a reason for your answer. This could be working to show the correct answer, or it could be providing a reason or a counter-example.

Worked examples and more!

TOP TIP
Tick any 'yes' or 'no' boxes as appropriate. If there aren't any boxes, state 'yes' or 'no' in your answer.

Example questions

1 Probability • Grade 1–3

A bag contains 10 red marbles, 6 green marbles and 4 blue marbles.
Flo says the probability of pulling a green marble from the bag is $\frac{1}{3}$ because there are three colours in the bag.

Is she correct?
Give a reason for your answer.

[1 mark]

2 Algebra • Grade 3–5

Jon says the only integer that satisfies $\quad 3 \leqslant x < 4 \quad$ is 3

Is he correct?
Give a reason for your answer.

[1 mark]

Complete the example

Volume of a pyramid = $\frac{1}{3}$ × base area × perpendicular height

Archie uses estimation and says the volume of this pyramid is at least 60 cm³

Is he correct?

Tick a box.

☐ Yes   ☑ No

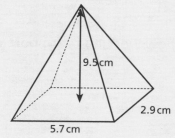

9.5 cm

2.9 cm

5.7 cm

Show working to support your answer.   **[3 marks]**

2.9 rounded to the nearest integer is ....

5.7 rounded to the nearest integer is ....

9.5 rounded to the nearest integer is ....

> Estimate the volume by rounding each dimension.

Estimate for the area of the base is .... cm × .... cm = ... cm²

Substituting the estimated values in the formula, $V = \frac{1}{3}$ × .... × .... = ... cm³

Each dimension has been rounded up to the nearest integer, so 60 cm³ is an

....

The volume cannot be .... than 60 cm³, so he is ....

Exam practice questions

 10

1

Talia converts $\frac{23}{5}$ to a mixed number.

She writes,

23 ÷ 5 = 4 remainder 3   so

$\frac{23}{5} = 3\frac{4}{5}$

Is she correct?

Tick a box.

☐ Yes   ☐ No

Show working to support your answer.   **[1 mark]**

....

....

Ratio, Proportion and Rates of Change • Grade 1–3 🔳

Safa says that $\frac{2}{3}$ of a day is less than 1000 minutes.

Is she correct?

Tick a box.

☐ Yes   ☐ No

You **must** show working to support your answer.   **[2 marks]**

Statistics • Grade 1–3 🔳

185 people were asked for their favourite ice cream flavour.
The bar chart shows the results.

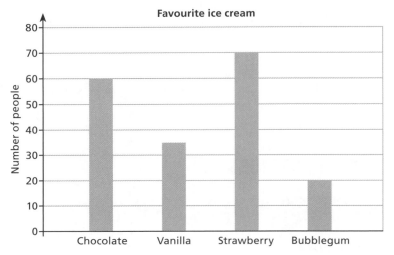

Favourite ice cream

Hendel says, "30 people said vanilla because the bar is half the height of the chocolate bar."

Is he correct?

Tick a box.

☐ Yes   ☐ No

Give a reason to support your answer.   **[1 mark]**

4 Geometry and Measures • Grade 3–5 ▦

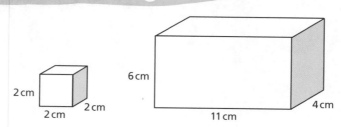

6 cm

2 cm

2 cm 2 cm

11 cm 4 cm

Clare says, "I can fit 33 cubes in the box because the volume of the box is 264 cm³. The volume of each cube is 8 cm³ and 264 ÷ 8 = 33."

Is she correct?

Give a reason for your answer.   [1 mark]

....

....

5 Number • Grade 3–5 ▦

Henry measures one side of a square table as 1.6 m to 1 decimal place.

He says the real length could be anywhere between 1.5 m and 1.7 m so the error interval is 1.5 m ⩽ length < 1.7 m

Is he correct?

Tick a box.

☐ Yes   ☐ No

Give a reason for your answer.   [2 marks]

....

....

....

....

6 Algebra • Grade 3–5 ▤

Evie says that $(a + 2)(a - 1) = a^2 - 2$ [2 marks]

Is she correct?

Show working to support your answer.

....

....

....

....

Total score: .... / 9

Use (a given method)

Use: A formula or fact may be given (e.g. a conversion) for you to use. You may be asked to use given data or a given graph to answer a question.

Use a given method (e.g. Pythagoras' theorem, complete the square): Use the stated method to find the answer.

Use approximations to: Round to 1 significant figure (unless told differently) and complete the calculation.

Use your calculator to: You can use your calculator to work out the answer in one step (but it is advisable to show any intermediate steps of working).

Worked example and more!

Use ruler and compasses: Construct the answer using a ruler and compasses, showing any construction arcs.

TOP TIP
Don't use another method unless the question states 'or otherwise'.

Example question

1   Ratio, Proportion and Rates of Change • Grade 1–3 🔢

Use 8 km = 5 miles to convert 35 miles to kilometres.   **[2 marks]**

Complete the example

<u>Use</u> trigonometry to work out the size of angle x.

[2 marks]

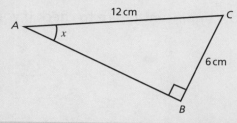

The lengths of the opposite side and the hypotenuse are given, so use sine. Remember:

$$\sin x = \frac{\text{opposite}}{\text{hypotenuse}} \qquad \cos x = \frac{\text{adjacent}}{\text{hypotenuse}} \qquad \tan x = \frac{\text{opposite}}{\text{adjacent}}$$

$$\sin x = \frac{\square}{12}$$

$$x = \sin^{-1}\left(\frac{\square}{\square}\right)$$

⬅ Make sure you know how to use the sin⁻¹ button on your calculator.

$$x = \underline{\hspace{2cm}} degrees$$

Exam practice questions

⏱ **30**

1

Here are some number cards.

a) Use **all** three cards so that the answer to the calculation is an odd number.   **[1 mark]**

b) Use **all** three cards so that the answer to the calculation is a multiple of 10   **[1 mark]**

c) Use **all** three cards so that the answer to the calculation is correct.   **[1 mark]**

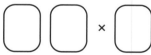

$$\frac{2 + \boxed{}}{\boxed{} + \boxed{}} = \frac{1}{2}$$

2 Number • Grade 1–3 🔢

a)   Use your calculator to work out the exact value of $\dfrac{2020.5 + 29.7}{10.2}$ **[1 mark]**

....

b)   Use approximations to 1 significant figure to check if your answer to part a) is sensible.

[3 marks]

....

....

....

3 Ratio, Proportion and Rates of Change • Grade 1–3 🔢

Use the height of the house to estimate the height of the mobile phone mast.   **[2 marks]**

7.5 m

.... m

4 Ratio, Proportion and Rates of Change • Grade 1–3 🔢

A map is drawn with a scale of 1 : 200 000

Use the scale to work out the actual distance represented by 6 cm on the map.
Give your answer in kilometres.   **[3 marks]**

.... km

5 Statistics • Grade 1–3 📟

Some students are asked about their favourite after-school clubs.

Football	◯◯◯
Gymnastics	◯◯◖
Dance	◯◯◯◯
Swimming	◯◯◯

◯ = 10 students

Use the pictogram to answer the following questions.

a) How many students are surveyed?   [1 mark]

....

b) Which activity is the most popular?   [1 mark]

....

c) Which **two** activities do an equal number of students prefer?   [1 mark]

.... and ....

6 Ratio, Proportion and Rates of Change • Grade 3–5 🖩

Here is a conversion graph between euros (€) and pounds (£).

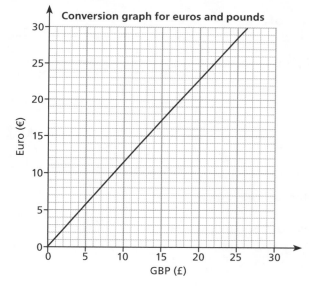

a) Use the graph to convert £20 to euros.   [1 mark]

€ ....

b) Use your answer to part a) to complete the conversion table.   [2 marks]

Pounds (£)	Euros (€)
10	
20	
40	

77

7 Geometry and Measures • Grade 3–5 ▦

Use Pythagoras' theorem to work out the length x.   **[3 marks]**

35 m

x

12 m

$x =$ .... m

8 Probability • Grade 3–5 ▦

Some teachers are asked if they like tea or coffee.

ξ = teachers surveyed
T = teachers who like tea
C = teachers who like coffee

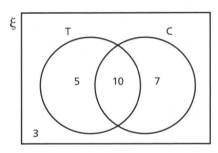

Use the Venn diagram to work out

a) the total number of teachers surveyed   **[1 mark]**

....

b) the number of teachers who do **not** like tea or coffee   **[1 mark]**

....

c) the number of teachers who like tea but do **not** like coffee   **[1 mark]**

....

9   Algebra • Grade 3–5 🔲

The graph of $y = x^2 + 2x - 3$ is shown.

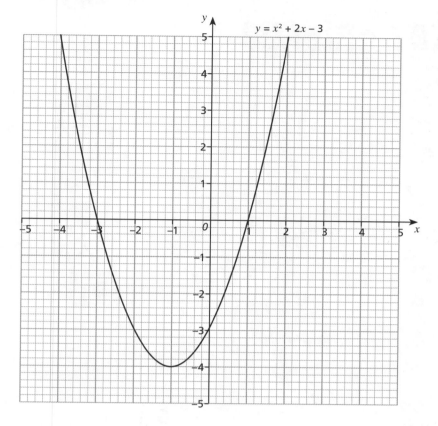

$y = x^2 + 2x - 3$

Use the graph to write down

a) the solutions of $x^2 + 2x - 3 = 0$ **[1 mark]**

.... and ....

b) the coordinates of the turning point   **[1 mark]**

(.................... , ...)

c) the coordinates of the y-intercept   **[1 mark]**

(.................... , ...)

10   Geometry and Measures • Grade 3–5 🔲

Use the triangles to work out the sum of the interior angles of a hexagon.   **[2 marks]**

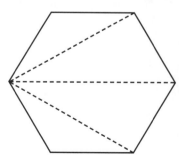

.... degrees

Total score: .... **/ 29**

Translate/Reflect/ Rotate/Enlarge

Translate: Draw the image in the correct position.

Reflect: Draw the mirror image of the object in the correct position.

Enlarge: Using the given scale factor, draw the image at the correct size. The image must also be in the correct position if you are given a centre of enlargement on a coordinate grid.

Worked example and more!

Rotate: Draw the image in the correct position and orientation.

Example question

1 Geometry and Measures • Grade 3–5 📟

Translate the trapezium by the vector $\begin{pmatrix} 4 \\ 3 \end{pmatrix}$ **[2 marks]**

TOP TIP
Use a ruler to draw the image accurately.

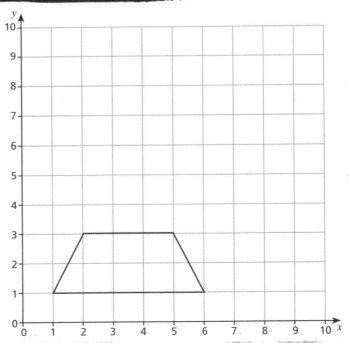

Complete the example

Reflect the pentagon in the line $x = 1$

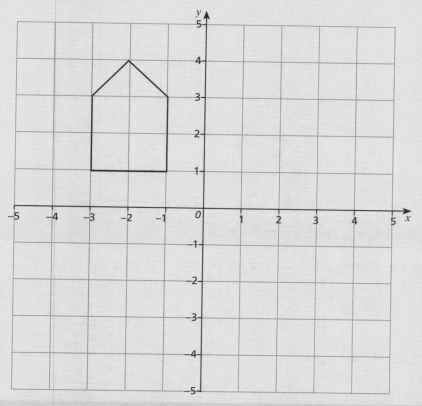

Draw the line $x = 1$ on the grid. Reflect each point across the line $x = 1$. Then connect the points. The shape in your answer must be congruent to the given shape.

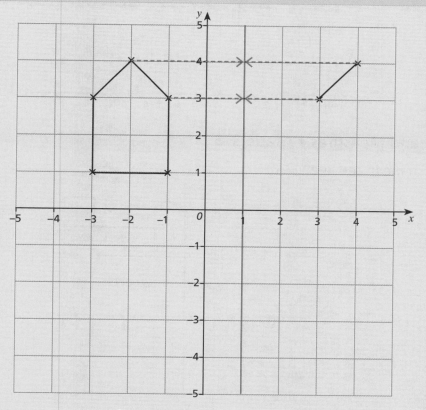

Exam practice questions

1 Geometry and Measures • Grade 1–3 🖩

On the grid, enlarge the triangle with a scale factor of 2

[2 marks]

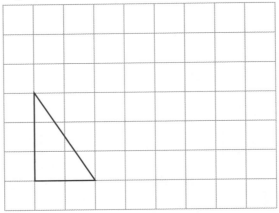

2 Geometry and Measures • Grade 1–3 🖩

Translate the parallelogram 1 square to the left and 3 squares up.

[2 marks]

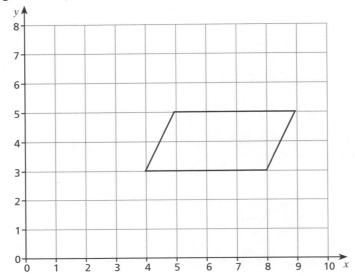

3 Geometry and Measures • Grade 3–5 🖩

Reflect the shape in the line $y = 1$

[2 marks]

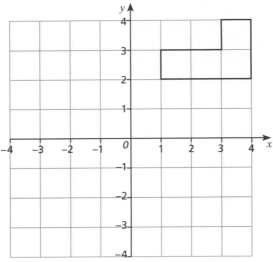

Geometry and Measures • Grade 3–5 📱

Rotate the kite 90° clockwise about the point (1, 2).

[2 marks]

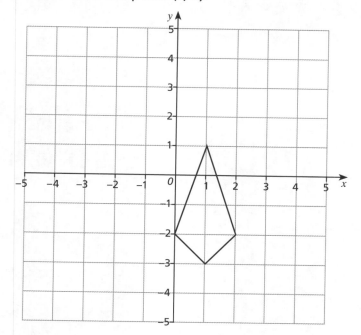

Geometry and Measures • Grade 3–5 📱

Enlarge the triangle by a scale factor of 3 about centre (0, 0).

[2 marks]

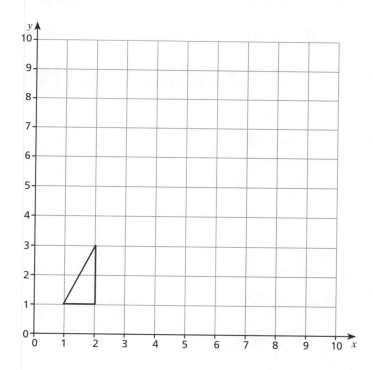

Total score: .... **/ 10**

Describe

Describe: Use mathematical words to describe, define or explain a given diagram, pattern or sequence.

Describe (fully) the single transformation that maps: Use mathematical words to state what single transformation has changed a shape on a coordinate grid.

Worked example and more!

Example question

1 Geometry and Measures • Grade 1–3 🔲

Describe fully the single transformation that maps triangle A onto triangle B.

[2 marks]

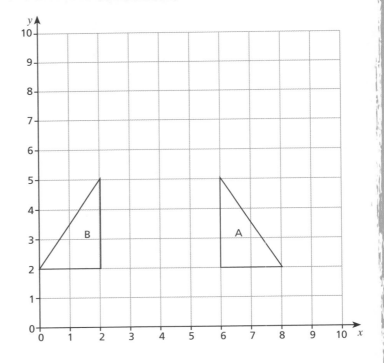

TOP TIP
'Describe fully' is a reminder that there is more than one part to the answer.

Complete the example

Here is a sequence.   −2, 1, 4, 7, 10

Describe the sequence by giving the nth term rule.   ← The nth term rule is sometimes called the position-to-term rule.   **[2 marks]**

$$-2 \quad 1 \quad 4 \quad 7 \quad 10$$
$$+3 \; + \underline{\quad} \; + \underline{\quad} \; + \underline{\quad}$$

Position	1	2	3	4	5	n
Term	−2	1	4	7	10	?
Times table	1 × 3 = 3	2 × 3 = 6	___ × 3 = 9	___ × 3 = ___	___ × ___ = ___	n × ___ = ___ n
Difference between the term and the times table	−2 − 3 = −5	1 − 6 = −5	4 − ___ = −5	7 − ___ = ___	___ − ___ = ___	

The nth term rule is _____

Exam practice questions

1 **Algebra • Grade 1–3**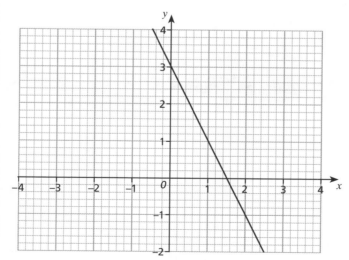

Here is a graph of a line.

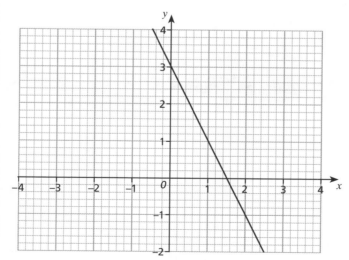

Describe the graph by inserting the words **positive** or **negative** into this statement.   **[1 mark]**

The line has a _____ gradient and the y-intercept is a _____ value.

Geometry and Measures • Grade 1–3 📖

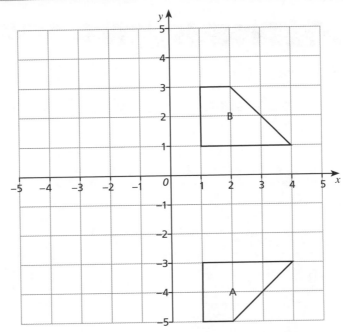

Describe **fully** the single transformation that maps quadrilateral A onto quadrilateral B.

[2 marks]

....

....

3

Algebra • Grade 3–5 📖

Here is a sequence.   1, 2, 3, 5, 8, 13

Describe the rule for continuing the sequence.

[1 mark]

....

....

4

Geometry and Measures • Grade 3–5 📖

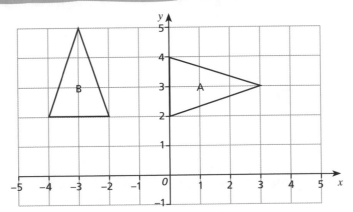

Describe **fully** the single transformation that maps shape A onto shape B.

[3 marks]

....

....

Statistics • Grade 3–5 🖩

Here is a scatter graph showing the number of ice creams sold compared to the temperature outside over 22 days.

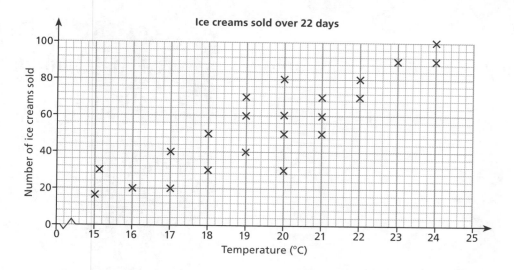

Describe the correlation between the number of ice creams sold and the outside temperature.

[1 mark]

....

....

6 **Geometry and Measures • Grade 3–5** 🖩

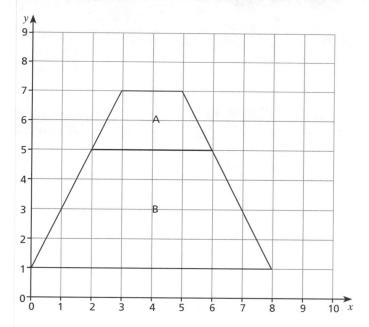

Describe **fully** the single transformation that maps shape A onto shape B. **[3 marks]**

....

....

Total score: .... **/ 11**

Construct

Worked examples and more!

TOP TIP
Remember to show all your construction lines and arcs, and make sure they are clear.

Example questions

1 Geometry and Measures • Grade 3–5

Construct the locus of points that are all 2 cm from a fixed point. **[1 mark]**

•

2 Geometry and Measures • Grade 3–5

Construct an equilateral triangle with side lengths of 6 cm. **[3 marks]**

Complete the example

Here is angle *ABC*.

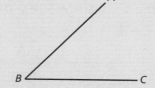

Construct the angle bisector of angle *ABC*.   [2 marks]

1. Put the point of the compasses on the vertex of
   .... and draw an arc intersecting
   .... and ....

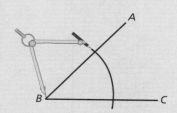

2. Put the point of the compasses on the intersection of
   the arc and ....
   Draw an arc in the middle of the angle.

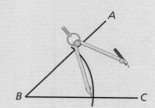

3. Keep the compasses the same distance apart.
   Repeat step 2 on the other intersection.

4. Line up the ruler and draw a line from the
   .... of the angle to the intersecting arcs
   from steps 2 and 3.

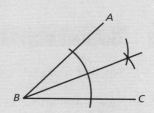

Exam practice questions

1

Using ruler and compasses, construct a triangle with sides 8 cm, 7 cm and 5 cm.
The 8 cm side has been drawn for you.   [2 marks]

_____

8 cm

Geometry and Measures • Grade 3–5 🖩

The map shows two towns, *A* and *B*.
Town *C* is less than 5 km from *A* and less than 4 km from *B*.

Construct **two** arcs to show the possible position of town *C*.
Label the region *R*.   **[3 marks]**

Key: 1 cm represents 1 km

Geometry and Measures • Grade 3–5 🖩

Here is a sketch of a rhombus.

Use ruler and compasses to construct an accurate
drawing of rhombus *ABCD*.
Show your construction lines clearly.
The diagonal has been drawn for you.

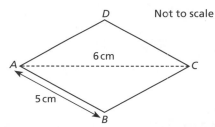

[3 marks]

A ———————————— *C*

4   Geometry and Measures • Grade 3–5 🖩

Use ruler and compasses to construct the perpendicular bisector of line segment *XY*.   **[2 marks]**

X ———————————————— Y

5   Geometry and Measures • Grade 3–5 🖩

You will need ruler and compasses for this question.
ABCD shows a drawing of a patio.

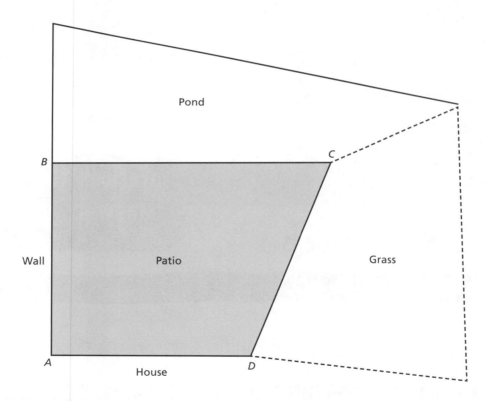

Tom wants to put a post on his patio.

He wants it to be closer to the grass than to the house.

Label the region, *R*, where the post could be placed.

Show your construction lines.

[3 marks]

Total score: _____ **/ 13**

Give your answer

Write the answer in a particular format, e.g. as a fraction, as a decimal, to a number of decimal places, in terms of π, in a particular unit.

Worked examples and more!

TOP TIP
Make sure you read the whole question. In exam conditions, it is easy to overlook the 'Give your answer...' instruction.

Example questions

1 Number • Grade 1–3

Work out $\frac{7}{8} + \frac{9}{10}$

Give your answer as a mixed number. [2 marks]

2 Geometry and Measures • Grade 3–5

A point is translated from (3, 6) to (0, 8).

Describe the translation.
Give your answer as a column vector. [2 marks]

Complete the example

The diagram shows a circle inside a square.

Work out the area of the shaded section.

Give your answer in terms of π.

[3 marks]

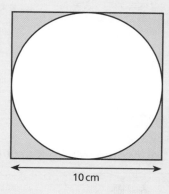

10 cm

Area of the circle is $\pi \times$ _____^{2} = _____ π cm^2

Area of the square is $10 \times 10 =$ _____ cm^2

Shaded area = (_____ − _____) cm^2

> The diameter of the circle is 10 cm.
> The radius is half of the diameter so radius = 5 cm
> The formula for the area of a circle is πr^2

Exam practice questions

1 Number • Grade 1–3 🖩

Work out $\frac{5}{2} \times \frac{3}{4}$

Give your answer as a mixed number.

[2 marks]

2 Geometry and Measures • Grade 1–3 🖩

A girl is facing West.

She turns through 90° anticlockwise.

What direction is she facing now?

Give your answer as a three-figure bearing.

[1 mark]

_____ °

3 Ratio, Proportion and Rates of Change • Grade 1–3 🖩

A box holds 12 000 tubs of yogurt.
Each tub contains 250 millilitres.

How much yogurt is in the box?
Give your answer in litres.

[2 marks]

.... litres

4 Probability • Grade 1–3 🖩

The table shows information about some workers arriving at a factory one day.

	Early	On time	Late
Number of workers	32	66	2

Use the information to estimate the probability that a worker, chosen at random, was late.
Give your answer as a decimal.

[2 marks]

....

5 Statistics • Grade 1–3 🖩

25 people raise £540.30 for charity.

Work out the mean amount raised per person.
Give your answer to the nearest penny.

[2 marks]

£ ....

6 Geometry and Measures • Grade 1–3 ▦

Work out the area of a circle of radius 4.5 cm
Give your answer to 1 decimal place.

[2 marks]

.... cm²

7 Algebra • Grade 3–5 ▦

Here is a formula to work out the cost, in pence, of an electricity bill:

$$C = 46d + 34k$$

where d is the number of days and k is the number of kilowatt hours (kWh)

Work out the bill if $d = 30$ and $k = 231$
Give your answer in pounds.

[3 marks]

£ ....

8 Ratio, Proportion and Rates of Change / Geometry and Measures • Grade 3–5 ▦

The circle shown has radius 8 cm
Area of sector X : Area of sector Y = 5 : 3

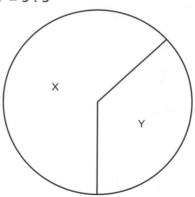

Work out the perimeter of sector Y.
Give your answer in terms of π.

[4 marks]

.... cm

9 Number / Ratio, Proportion and Rates of Change • Grade 3–5 🔳

An electric car covers a quarter mile in 12 seconds.

Hint: 12 seconds is one-fifth of a minute

Work out the average speed of the car.
Give your answer in miles per hour (mph).

[2 marks]

.... mph

10 Number • Grade 3–5 🔳

Use your calculator to work out $\sqrt{82.7} + 4.1^2$
Give your answer to 2 decimal places.

[2 marks]

....

11 Algebra / Geometry and Measures • Grade 3–5 🔳

The diagram shows a triangle.

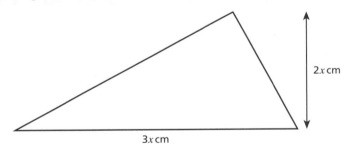

2x cm

3x cm

Work out an expression for the area of the triangle.
Give your answer in its simplest form.

[2 marks]

.... cm²

The diagram shows a cuboid.

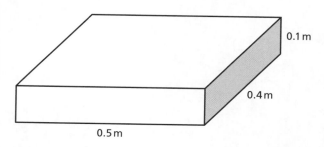

0.1 m

0.4 m

0.5 m

a) Work out the area of **one** of the smallest faces.

Give your answer in square centimetres.

[2 marks]

.... cm²

b) Work out the volume of the cuboid.

Give your answer in cubic centimetres.

[2 marks]

.... cm³

Total score: .... **/ 28**

Give a reason/an example

Give a reason: Show a calculation, written evidence or an explanation to support your answer or a given statement.

Give an example: Write an example to support or to disprove a given answer, a piece of working or a given statement.

Worked examples and more!

TOP TIP
These questions test the depth of your knowledge so make sure you work on any topics you feel less confident about.

Example questions

1 Statistics • Grade 1–3

Ten students take an exam. Here are their marks.

8   12   22   22   35   47   50   50   50   50

Give a reason why the mode is **not** the best average to use.   **[1 mark]**

2 Number • Grade 3–5

Pieces of wood are cut into 2-metre lengths to the nearest 10 cm.

Give an example to show that two pieces could have a total length of 3.9 metres.   **[2 marks]**

Complete the example

A roll of plain wallpaper is 10 metres long to the nearest metre.
Jon says, "I might be able to cut four pieces from the roll that are each 2.6 metres long."

Give an example to show that he could be correct.

[2 marks]

The error interval for the roll is _____ m ⩽ length < _____ m

The total length of the four pieces is 4 × 2.6 = _____ m

This is within the error interval so he could be correct.

Exam practice questions

1   Number • Grade 1–3

Kaleb is working out this calculation.   8 ÷ 2 + 3 × 4

He writes,   8 ÷ 2 = 4   4 + 3 = 7   7 × 4 = 28   so the answer is 28

Is his method correct?
Give a reason for your answer.

[2 marks]

2   Algebra • Grade 1–3

A sequence of patterns is made using black triangles and white triangles.

     Pattern 1   Pattern 2   Pattern 3   Pattern 4

a)   Will the number of black triangles in a pattern always be a triangular number?
     Give a reason for your answer.

[1 mark]

b)   Pattern 99 has 4950 black triangles.

     How many white triangles are in Pattern 100?
     Give a reason for your answer.

[1 mark]

3 Probability • Grade 1–3

The probabilities of Easy, Medium and Hard questions in a quiz are shown in the table.
The quiz has three rounds. In each round the questions are chosen at random.

	Easy	Medium	Hard
Round 1	0.7	0.2	0.1
Round 2	0.5	0.3	0.2
Round 3	0.4	0.3	0.3

Which of these is most likely?

A   Getting an Easy question in Round 1

B   Getting a question that is **not** Hard in Round 2

C   Getting a question that is Medium or Hard in Round 3

Give a reason for your answer.   **[2 marks]**

....

....

4 Algebra • Grade 1–3

Give a reason why *ABC* should be a straight line.   **[1 mark]**

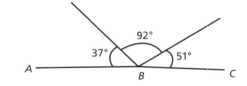

....

5 Algebra / Geometry and Measures • Grade 3–5

The diagram shows a triangle.

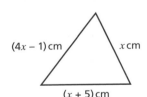

When $x = 2$, what type of triangle is shown?
Give a reason for your answer.   **[2 marks]**

....

....

6 Probability • Grade 3–5

Ava throws an ordinary coin 5 times. It lands on heads every time.
She says, "Next time I throw it, it must land on tails."

Give a reason why she could be wrong.   **[1 mark]**

....

7 Statistics • Grade 3–5 🔲

The table shows the heights of 50 students.

Height, h (metres)	$1.2 \leqslant h < 1.4$	$1.4 \leqslant h < 1.6$	$1.6 \leqslant h < 1.8$	$1.8 \leqslant h < 2.0$
Frequency	3	24	18	5

Ahmed says, "The median height is 1.6 metres."

Give a reason why he **must** be incorrect.

[1 mark]

....

8 Algebra • Grade 3–5 🔲

Two identical jugs are being filled with water, starting at the same time, as shown.

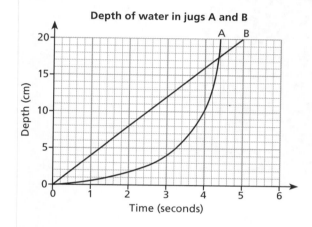

a) Which jug is being filled at a constant rate?
Give a reason for your answer.

[2 marks]

....

....

b) Which jug is full first?
Give a reason for your answer.

[2 marks]

....

....

9 Geometry and Measures • Grade 3–5 🔲

Give a reason why these triangles are congruent.

[1 mark]

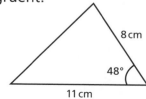 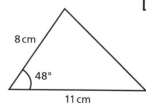

Total score: .... / 16

Criticise/Identify any mistakes/What error?

Worked example and more!

Identify any mistakes or errors in a piece of working, a method or a calculation.

TOP TIP
Work step-by-step through the given information to spot what's wrong or inaccurate.

Example question

1   **Geometry and Measures • Grade 3–5** 🖩

A student wants to find the midpoint of *AB* using a construction.

This is her method:

    Make two arcs of equal radius from *A* and *D*.

    Draw a line through the intersections of the arcs.

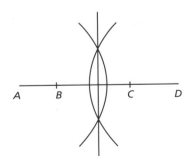

What error has she made?

[1 mark]

Complete the example

The graph shows the distance travelled by a van driver on four different days.

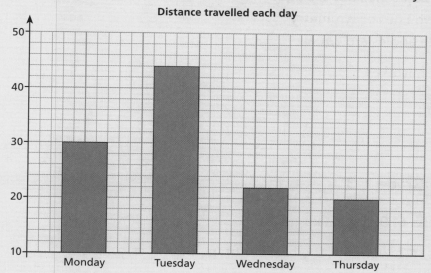

Make **two** **criticisms** of the graph.   **[2 marks]**

1   The vertical scale should start at ....

2   The vertical scale also needs a .... (e.g. ....).

Exam practice questions

⏱ 12

1

This question is given to a student.

     Simplify fully $8x - 7 - (3x - 2)$

     She writes, $8x - 7 - (3x - 2) = 8x - 7 - 3x - 2$
                                         $= 5x + 9$

Identify any mistakes she has made.   **[2 marks]**

2 Geometry and Measures • Grade 1–3 🖩

Amaya is trying to describe a kite.

- It has four sides
- Pairs of adjacent sides are equal
- It has two lines of symmetry
- Opposite angles are equal

Correct her mistakes.   **[2 marks]**

....

....

3 Number • Grade 1–3 🖩

Yoghurt costs £1.95 for a 1 kg tub.

a) Jo says, "To work out the cost per gram, do this calculation."

$$£1.95 ÷ 100$$

What error has she made?   **[1 mark]**

....

b) Kai says, "To work out the number of grams per penny, do this calculation."

$$(1000 ÷ 1.95) \text{ grams}$$

What error has he made?   **[1 mark]**

....

4 Ratio, Proportion and Rates of Change • Grade 1–3 🖩

Jack is asked to increase £300 by 2%

He writes,   £300 × 1.2 = £360

What mistake has he made?   **[1 mark]**

....

....

5 Geometry and Measures • Grade 3–5

Kim is asked to draw the locus of points that are 2 metres from the bar shown.

This is her answer.

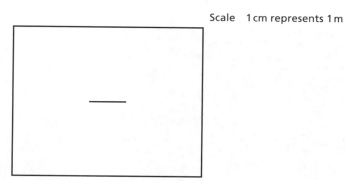

Scale   1 cm represents 1 m

Criticise her answer.   [1 mark]

....

....

6 Geometry and Measures • Grade 3–5

Luka is trying to work out the length x to 1 decimal place.

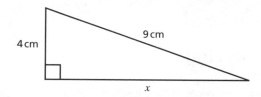

4 cm

9 cm

x

He writes,

$x^2 = 4^2 + 9^2$

$x^2 = 8 + 18$

$x^2 = 26$

$x = \sqrt{26}$, $x = 5.1$ cm (1 d.p.)

Identify any mistakes he has made and then give the correct answer.   [3 marks]

....

....

....

.... cm

Total score: .... / 11

Compare

Worked example and more!

Find similarities or differences between two or more calculations, graphs, facts or statements (e.g. identify which is larger or smaller, faster or slower).

TOP TIP
Make sure you take into account the context of the question in your comparison.

Example question

1 **Probability • Grade 1–3** 🖩

Bags A and B contain red discs and yellow discs.
Bag A contains twice as many red discs as yellow discs.
Bag B contains 15 red discs and 5 yellow discs.

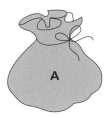

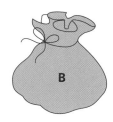

A disc is chosen at random from each bag.

Compare the probability of getting a red disc from bag A with the probability of getting a red disc from bag B.

[3 marks]

Complete the example

Compare the values of each of the following.

50% of £50

$\frac{3}{5}$ of £40

0.7 × £30

You **must** show your working.   **[3 marks]**

50% of £50 = $\frac{1}{2}$ × £50 $\frac{3}{5}$ of £40 = $\frac{3}{5}$ × £40   0.7 × £30 = £........................

= £........................   = £........................

So in order of value, starting from the smallest.

.... , ... , ...

Exam practice questions

1 **Geometry and Measures • Grade 1–3**

The diagram shows a rectangle and a square.

3 cm

8 cm

5.5 cm

a) Compare the areas.   **[2 marks]**

....

....

b) Compare the perimeters.   **[2 marks]**

....

....

2 Number • Grade 3–5 ▦

The table shows information about the students in a school.

	Number of students	Median age (years)	Proportion of all students with special needs
Boys	442	13.6	6.8% (1 d.p.)
Girls	408	14.0	7.5% (1 d.p.)

Compare the boys and the girls at this school.   **[3 marks]**
The headings are to help you.

Percentage of boys and girls.

....

Average age

....

Numbers with special needs

....

3 Statistics • Grade 3–5 ▦

The table shows information about the amounts that 40 people spend getting to and from work each day.

Amount, A (£)	Midpoint	Frequency	
$0 \leqslant A < 10$		23	
$10 \leqslant A < 20$		14	
$20 \leqslant A < 30$		3	

The average British worker spends about £8.50 on getting to and from work.

Compare the mean amounts for these 40 people and the average British worker.   **[4 marks]**

....

....

....

....

You are given that

$$\text{Pressure} = \frac{\text{Force}}{\text{Area}}$$

The table shows the forces being applied to the areas of two objects, A and B.

	Force (N)	Area (m²)
Object A	120	0.5
Object B	180	1.5

Compare the pressures on each object.   **[3 marks]**

....

....

....

....

Total score:.................... **/ 14**

Show (that)

Write your workings to clarify how you chose an answer, so it is clear that you are not guessing.

Worked examples and more!

TOP TIP
Show the methods that you are using to prove the statement.

Example questions

1 Number • Grade 1–3

Jack says that   2.6 ÷ 0.5 = 1.3

Show that he is incorrect.

[1 mark]

2 Geometry and Measures • Grade 3–5

ABC and ADE are straight lines.

BD is parallel to CE.

Show that x is an acute angle.   [3 marks]

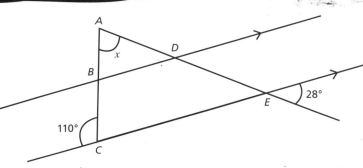

Complete the example

Show that there are four prime numbers less than 100 that are 1 more than a square number.

[2 marks]

Listing the square numbers up to 100 gives 1, 4, 9, ……, ……, ……, ……, ……, ……, 100

Listing the numbers that are 1 more than the square numbers gives

2, 5, 10, ……, ……, ……, ……, ……, ……, 101

The prime numbers less than 100 in this list are 2, 5, …… and ……

There are four prime numbers less than 100 in the list.

Exam practice questions

(28)

1 Number • Grade 1–3

A fair six-sided spinner is spun twice.
The score is the sum of the numbers it lands on.

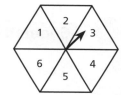

Show that there are six ways of getting a score of 7

[2 marks]

2 Geometry and Measures • Grade 1–3

Show that the regular shape with an interior angle of 120° is a hexagon.

[2 marks]

3 Number • Grade 1–3

Which of these fractions has the closest value to $\frac{3}{4}$?

$\frac{5}{8}$ $\frac{13}{20}$ $\frac{2}{3}$ $\frac{4}{5}$

Show working to support your answer.

[2 marks]

4 Statistics • Grade 1–3 🔢

The pictogram shows information about the favourite car colours of some students.

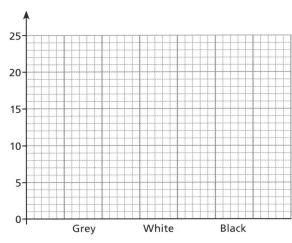

Grey	◯◯◯◯
White	◯◯◯◖
Black	◯◯◯◯◯◗

Key: ◯ represents 4 students

Show the information on a bar chart.   **[3 marks]**

5 Geometry and Measures • Grade 1–3 🔢

A car tyre has diameter of 60 cm.

a) Show that the circumference is 190 cm to the nearest 10 centimetres.   **[2 marks]**

....

....

b) Show that the tyre will rotate more than 500 times in travelling 1 km.   **[3 marks]**

....

....

....

6 Geometry and Measures • Grade 1–3 🔢

The diagram shows a prism with volume 150 cm³

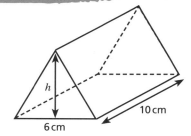

Show that $h = 5$ cm   **[2 marks]**

....

....

....

7 Ratio, Proportion and Rates of Change • Grade 3–5 🔢

There are 52 playing cards in a pack.
The cards are put into two piles in the ratio 8 : 5

Show that there are 12 more cards in the first pile than the second pile. **[3 marks]**

8 Algebra • Grade 3–5 🔢

Show clearly that the lines $y = 7 - 3x$ and $6x + 2y = 6$ are parallel. **[3 marks]**

9 Probability • Grade 3–5 🔢

Here are six cards.

15   18   10   16   10   9

Show that mode < median < mean **[3 marks]**

10 Probability • Grade 3–5 🔢

A student is asked to draw a rectangle with side lengths that are whole centimetres and an area of 20 cm²

Show that the probability that the rectangle has perimeter 18 cm is $\frac{1}{3}$ **[3 marks]**

Total score: _____ / 28

Mixed Questions

1 Geometry and Measures • Grade 1–3 🖩

a) Complete the table so that the lengths in each row are equal.

[2 marks]

Millimetres (mm)	Centimetres (cm)	Metres (m)	Kilometres (km)
9000		9	
	6		0.00006

b) Rob says that   6 cm + 9 m is 9.6 m

Is he correct?

Tick a box.   ☐ Yes   ☐ No

You **must** show working to support your answer.

[1 mark]

....

....

2 Geometry and Measures • Grade 1–3 🖩

Here is a grid showing the points *A*, *B*, *C*, *D* and *E*.

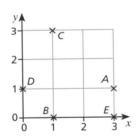

a) Match each pair of coordinates to the correct letter.
One has been done for you.

[3 marks]

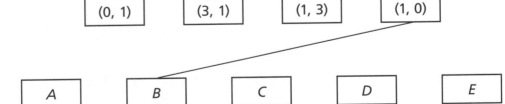

b) Which four of the points, when joined, form a trapezium?
Give **two** possible answers.

[2 marks]

....

....

3 Algebra • Grade 1–3 🖩

The equation of a straight line is $y = 3x - 3$

a) Write down the coordinates of the y-intercept.

[1 mark]

(............. , ...)

b) Write down the gradient of the line.

[1 mark]

....

c) Which of the following lines is parallel to the line $y = 3x - 3$?
Circle your answer.

[1 mark]

$2y + 6x = 8$ $2y - 6x = 8$ $6y + 2x = 8$ $6y - 2x = 8$

4 Number • Grade 1–3 🖩

a) Show that $\frac{5}{9}$ is greater than $\frac{1}{2}$ and less than $\frac{4}{7}$

[2 marks]

....

....

b) What is the reciprocal of $\frac{5}{9}$?

Give your answer as a mixed number.

[2 marks]

....

5 Ratio, Proportion and Rates of Change / Geometry and Measures • Grade 1–3 🖩

The diagram shows an equilateral triangle and a square.

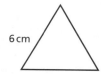 

6 cm   5 cm

a) Write the ratio **perimeter of triangle : perimeter of square** in its simplest form.   [2 marks]

....

b) The lengths of the square are decreased by 10%.

Work out the new ratio **perimeter of triangle : perimeter of square** in its simplest form.

[3 marks]

....

6 Ratio, Proportion and Rates of Change • Grade 3–5 🔢

a) Pink paint is made by mixing red and white paint in the ratio 2 : 7

What fraction of the paint is white?
Circle your answer.

[1 mark]

$$\frac{2}{7} \qquad \frac{5}{7} \qquad \frac{2}{9} \qquad \frac{7}{9}$$

b) The pink paint covers 13 square metres per litre.
Each wall of a square room measures 4.7 m by 3 m

How many litres of pink paint are needed to cover the walls with two coats of paint?
Give your answer to the nearest litre.

[4 marks]

.... litres

7 Number • Grade 3–5 🔢

a) Write 180 as a product of prime factors.

[2 marks]

....

b) In prime factor form $\quad 600 = 2^3 \times 3 \times 5^2$

Use this to write down the highest common factor of 180 and 600
Give your answer in index form.

[1 mark]

....

8 Number • Grade 3–5 🔢

a) Work out the exact value of $\quad (4.3 + 7.1) \times 101$

[2 marks]

....

b) Use approximations to check whether your answer is sensible.

[2 marks]

....
....

A five-sided spinner is spun 100 times.

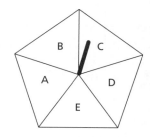

The table shows the number of times it lands on each letter.

Spinner lands on	A	B	C	D	E
Number of times	15	21	26	19	19

a) Do you think the spinner is fair?
   Give a reason for your answer.   **[1 mark]**

....

....

b) Work out the relative frequency of landing on A.   **[1 mark]**

....

10 **Algebra • Grade 3–5**

a) I think of a number.
   I double it and add 3
   My answer is 39

   Write down an equation to describe this.   **[1 mark]**

....

b) Solve your equation to work out the number I was thinking of.   **[2 marks]**

....

11 Statistics • Grade 3–5 🔲

The times that 100 passengers wait at a train station are shown.

Time, t (minutes)	$0 \leqslant t < 5$	$5 \leqslant t < 10$	$10 \leqslant t < 15$	$15 \leqslant t < 20$	$20 \leqslant t < 25$
Frequency	43	24	17	11	5

a) Which class interval contains the median? **[1 mark]**

b) Harley says that the range is 23 minutes.

Give an example to show that he could be correct. **[2 marks]**

12 Ratio, Proportion and Rates of Change • Grade 3–5 🔲

£3000 is invested at 4% compound interest.
The interest is added at the end of each year.

a) How much is the investment worth after 2 years? **[2 marks]**

£ ....

b) £6000 is invested for 1 year at 4% interest.

Which statement is correct, when compared with the investment above?
Tick a box.

This investment earns less interest ☐

This investment earns the same interest ☐

This investment earns more interest ☐

Give a reason for your answer. **[1 mark]**

13 Statistics • Grade 3–5

The table shows the time taken and the distance travelled by a delivery driver for 10 journeys.

Distance (miles)	2.4	8.5	6.0	19.9	3.8	6.2	10.0	18.5	13.0	17.0
Time (minutes)	9	15	12	27	8	13	17	24	17	20

a)   On the grid, draw a scatter diagram for this information.   **[3 marks]**

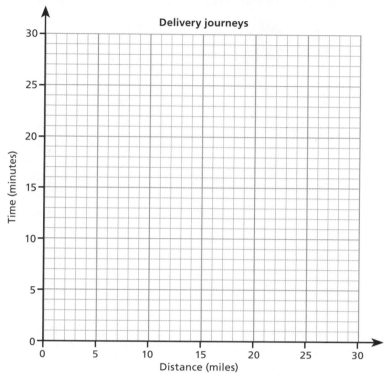

b)   Draw a line of best fit on your diagram.   **[1 mark]**

c)   A journey is 15 miles long.

How many minutes would you expect it to take?   **[1 mark]**

.... minutes

14 Algebra • Grade 3–5

a)   Factorise $x^2 - 5x - 36$ **[2 marks]**

....

b)   Use your answer to part a) to solve $x^2 - 5x - 36 = 0$ **[1 mark]**

$x =$ .... or $x =$ ....

Total score: .... / 51

Index of Topics

This index tells you which questions in this book offer practice for each of the six specification topics.

Topic	Page	Question	Example question	Complete the example	Exam practice question
Number	4	1	✓		
	6	3			✓
	6	7			✓
	8	1	✓		
	9	1			✓
	10	3			✓
	11	5			✓
	11	7			✓
	14	1	✓		
	15	1			✓
	16	3			✓
	20	1	✓		
	21	1			✓
	21	2			✓
	22	5			✓
	23	6			✓
	25	13			✓
	27	1			✓
	28	3			✓
	29	5			✓
	30	10			✓
	31	11			✓
	31	12			✓
	32	1	✓		
	33	1			✓
	33	2			✓
	36	2	✓		
	38	4			✓
	53	1			✓
	54	3			✓
	55	6			✓
	58	4			✓
	60	1	✓		
	61	1			✓
	71	1			✓
	73	5			✓
	75	1			✓
	76	2			✓
	92	1	✓		
	93	1			✓
	96	9			✓
	96	10			✓
	98	2	✓		
	99			✓	

Topic	Page	Question	Example question	Complete the example	Exam practice question
Number (cont.)	99	1			✓
	104	3			✓
	108	2			✓
	110	1	✓		
	111			✓	
	111	1			✓
	111	3			✓
	115	4			✓
	116	7			✓
	116	8			✓
Algebra	4	2	✓		
	5			✓	
	6	6			✓
	7	9			✓
	7	10			✓
	11	5			✓
	11	6			✓
	17	6			✓
	19	9			✓
	22	4			✓
	23	7			✓
	28	2			✓
	34	7			✓
	36	1	✓		
	37	1			✓
	38	2			✓
	38	5			✓
	39	6			✓
	39	7			✓
	39	8			✓
	40	1	✓		
	40	2	✓		
	41			✓	
	41	1			✓
	41	2			✓
	42	3			✓
	42	4			✓
	42	5			✓
	42	6			✓
	43	7			✓
	43	8			✓
	43	9			✓
	44	1	✓		
	44	2	✓		
	45			✓	

Topic	Page	Question	Example question	Complete the example	Exam practice question
Algebra (cont.)	45	1			✓
	46	2			✓
	46	3			✓
	46	4			✓
	47	5			✓
	47	6			✓
	47	7			✓
	48	1	✓		
	48	2	✓		
	49			✓	
	49	1			✓
	50	2			✓
	50	3			✓
	50	4			✓
	50	5			✓
	51	6			✓
	51	7			✓
	51	8			✓
	51	9			✓
	52	1	✓		
	55	5			✓
	55	7			✓
	59	6			✓
	59	7			✓
	61			✓	
	63	6			✓
	64	1	✓		
	68	5			✓
	69	8			✓
	70	2	✓		
	73	6			✓
	79	9			✓
	85			✓	
	85	1			✓
	86	3			✓
	95	7			✓
	96	11			✓
	99	2			✓
	100	4			✓
	100	5			✓
	101	8			✓
	103	1			✓
	113	8			✓
	115	3			✓
	117	10			✓
	119	14			✓
Ratio, Proportion and Rates of Change	6	5			✓
	10	2			✓
	12	8			✓
	14	2	✓		
	17	5			✓
	18	7			✓
	19	11			✓
	21			✓	

Topic	Page	Question	Example question	Complete the example	Exam practice question
Ratio, Proportion and Rates of Change (cont.)	24	11			✓
	25	12			✓
	29	7			✓
	30	9			✓
	32	2	✓		
	33			✓	
	33	3			✓
	34	4			✓
	34	5			✓
	34	6			✓
	35	8			✓
	35	9			✓
	37			✓	
	38	3			✓
	52	2	✓		
	54	4			✓
	59	8			✓
	67	3			✓
	72	2			✓
	74	1	✓		
	76	3			✓
	76	4			✓
	77	6			✓
	94	3			✓
	95	8			✓
	96	9			✓
	104	4			✓
	107			✓	
	109	4			✓
	113	7			✓
	115	5			✓
	116	6			✓
	118	12			✓
Geometry and Measures	5	1			✓
	6	4			✓
	9			✓	
	10	4			✓
	13	11			✓
	15			✓	
	18	8			✓
	19	10			✓
	20	2	✓		
	24	9			✓
	24	10			✓
	26	2	✓		
	27			✓	
	28	4			✓
	29	5			✓
	29	6			✓
	30	8			✓
	39	7			✓
	39	8			✓
	43	7			✓
	53			✓	

Topic	Page	Question	Example question	Complete the example	Exam practice question
Geometry and Measures (cont.)	54	2			✓
	64	1	✓		
	66	1			✓
	67	4			✓
	68	6			✓
	71			✓	
	73	4			✓
	75			✓	
	78	7			✓
	79	10			✓
	80	1	✓		
	81			✓	
	82	1			✓
	82	2			✓
	82	3			✓
	83	4			✓
	83	5			✓
	84	1	✓		
	86	2			✓
	86	4			✓
	87	6			✓
	88	1	✓		
	88	2	✓		
	89			✓	
	89	1			✓
	90	2			✓
	90	3			✓
	91	4			✓
	91	5			✓
	92	2	✓		
	93			✓	
	93	2			✓
	95	6			✓
	95	8			✓
	96	11			✓
	97	12			✓
	100	5			✓
	101	9			✓
	102	1	✓		
	104	2			✓
	105	5			✓
	105	6			✓
	107	1			✓
	110	2	✓		
	111	2			✓
	112	5			✓
	112	6			✓
	114	1			✓
	114	2			✓
	115	5			✓

Topic	Page	Question	Example question	Complete the example	Exam practice question
Probability	5	2			✓
	13	10			✓
	17	4			✓
	25	14			✓
	29	7			✓
	57			✓	
	57	1			✓
	58	3			✓
	62	2			✓
	70	1	✓		
	78	8			✓
	94	4			✓
	100	3			✓
	100	6			✓
	106	1	✓		
	113	9			✓
	113	10			✓
	117	9			✓
Statistics	7	8			✓
	8	2	✓		
	12	9			✓
	16	2			✓
	21	3			✓
	23	8			✓
	26	1	✓		
	39	6			✓
	56	1	✓		
	57	2			✓
	58	5			✓
	62	3			✓
	62	4			✓
	63	5			✓
	65			✓	
	66	2			✓
	69	7			✓
	72	3			✓
	77	5			✓
	87	5			✓
	94	5			✓
	98	1	✓		
	101	7			✓
	103			✓	
	108	3			✓
	112	4			✓
	118	11			✓
	119	13			✓

Answers

Pages 4–7: Write (down)

Complete the example

From *A* to *B* is 8 across and 4 up, so halfway from *A* to *B* is **4** across and **2** up.

So the midpoint of *AB* has coordinates **(2, 0)**.

Exam practice questions

1.

	Metric unit	
Length of a classroom	Metres (m)	[1]
Mass of a person	Kilograms (kg)	[1]
Amount of water in a large bottle	Litres (l) or centilitres (cl)	[1]

2. $\frac{1}{6}$ [1]
3. −3.5°C, −2.1°C, 0°C, 0.5°C [1]
4. 47 degrees [1]
5. 450 : 150 [1]
   3 : 1 [1]
6. a) 10 [1]
   4 [1]
   b) Subtract 6 or −6 [1]
7. $2^{10} (\div 2^3)$ [1]
   $= 2^7$ [1]
8. a) 2 [1]
   b) $\frac{3}{22}$ [1]
9. a) 4.9 [1]
   b) $\frac{1}{3}$ [1]
   c) $5b^2$ [2]
   [1 mark for 5 or b^2]
10. $2^2 + 6 \times 2 = 2 \times 8$ [2]
    [1 mark for each side]

Pages 8–13: Which / What / When

Complete the example

a) **A** and **C** are congruent
b) **B** and **G** are similar

Exam practice questions

1. 50p, 20p, 5p, 2p, 1p [1]
2. 5.5 m [2]
   [1 mark for 11 × 0.5]
3. a) 25% [1]
   b) 0.6 [1]
   c) $\frac{13}{20}$ [2]
   [1 mark for $\frac{65}{100}$]
4. Kite [2]
   [1 mark for a shape that satisfies one of the criteria, e.g. rhombus, square, rectangle]
5. a) Arithmetic or linear [1]
   b) 7, 13, 19 [2]
   [1 mark for any two correct and none incorrect]

6. a) Pattern 12 [1]
   b) Pattern 5 [2]
   [1 mark for 9 + 16 or 25 tiles]
7. 2 o'clock [2]
   [1 mark for LCM of 15 and 8 is 120]
8. Pack of 6 is best value with all comparisons shown [4]
   e.g. comparing cost of 12 rolls
   £2.95 × 6 = £17.70
   £5.40 × 3 = £16.20
   £6.99 × 2 = £13.98
   [3 marks for suitable comparisons of all three packs; 2 marks for comparing two packs and correct conclusion for those two packs; 1 mark for comparing two packs without a conclusion]
9. a) Wednesday (240) [2]
   [1 mark for at least three correct totals: Mon 110 + 140 = 250; Tue 140 + 110 = 250; Wed 40 + 200 = 240; Thu 180 + 70 = 250; Fri 290 + 180 = 470; Sat 180 + 210 = 390]
   b) Wednesday (160) [2]
   [1 mark for at least three correct differences: Mon 140 − 110 = 30; Tue 140 − 110 = 30; Wed 200 − 40 = 160; Thu 180 − 70 = 110; Fri 290 − 180 = 110; Sat 210 − 180 = 30]
10. 5 and 7 [3]
    [1 mark for stating either that two primes were removed or that two primes are remaining; 1 mark for stating that 1, 2, 3 and 6 must be remaining]
11 *EF* and *GH* with reason, e.g. alternate angles [2]
   [e.g. 1 mark for 180 − 70 − 78 = 32 or 70 + 78 = 148 (so *AB* and *CD* not parallel)]

Pages 14–19: How… long / many / much / does

Complete the example

a) 3 m = **300** cm
   To work out the number of small boxes that fit along the length, divide **300** cm by 50 cm. This gives **6** small boxes across the length.
   1 m = **100** cm
   To work out the number of small boxes that fit to the height and the width of the large box, divide **100** cm by 25 cm. This gives **4** small boxes in height and **4** small boxes across the width.
   The total number of small boxes that will fit inside the large box is **6 × 4 × 4 = 96**
b) Ana will be able to fit **more** small boxes into the large box.

Exam practice questions

1. £66.50 ÷ 7 [1]
   = £9.50 [1]
2. a) 5 [1]
   b) 33 teas sold, 22 coffees sold, so 33 − 22 [1]
   = 11 [1]

3. a) 26 [1]
    b) The fraction would get bigger/increase *or*
        He has now won 29 games out of 42 *or* sight of $\frac{29}{42}$ [1]
                                                                        [2]
4. 48
    [1 mark for calculating 12 red counters]
5. 855 ml or 0.855 l [3]
    **[1 mark for 1200 or 1.2 or 1200 − 345 or 1.2 − 0.345;
    1 mark for 855 or 0.855]**
6. a) 4 × 4 or 16 [1]
    b) 10^2 or 100 [1]
7. a) 45 minutes [3]
        **[1 mark for 30 ÷ 40; 1 mark for 0.75 hr; 1 mark for
        correct conversion to 45 minutes]**
    b) It will take him longer **or** it will take more time [1]
8. 9.1 m [3]
    **[1 mark for 8.75^2 or 76.5625 and 2.5^2 or 6.25 or
    82.8125; 1 mark for $\sqrt{(8.75^2 + 2.5^2)}$ or
    $\sqrt{(76.5625 + 6.25)}$ or $\sqrt{(82.8125)}$]**
9. 13 cm [4]
    **[1 mark for $x + 7$ or $2(x + 7)$ with any unknown;
    1 mark for $x + x + 7 + 2(x + 7) = 73$; 1 mark for
    $4x + 21 = 73$]**
10. 4 cm [2]
    [1 mark for 96 ÷ 6 or 16]
11. 30 [3]
    **[1 mark for ratio of goats to cows to sheep 5 : 4 : 6;
    1 mark for calculating multiplier of 6]**
    Alternative method:
    36 sheep so 24 cows (36 ÷ 3 × 2)
    Goats = 24 ÷ 4 × 5 = 30

Pages 20–25: Work out
Complete the example
One hour = **60** minutes
The car travels: 4.5 kilometres in 10 minutes
                  9 kilometres in 20 minutes
                  13.5 kilometres in 30 minutes
                  27 kilometres in 60 minutes
The average speed is **27** km/h.
Exam practice questions
1. 25 [1]
2. 1482 [3]
    **[1 mark for 342 or 1140 with the correct placing of 0
    for the multiplication by 20 or 182 or 1300 with the
    correct placing of 0 for the multiplication by 50 or for
    three correct numbers in a grid; 1 mark for adding the
    parts of the multiplication from the previous mark]**
3. 6 [2]
    [1 mark for ordering numbers 2, 3, 5, 7, 8, 9]
4. a) 7.5 cm [2]
        [1 mark for $4x = 30$]
    b) $10y$ [1]

5. £1.90 [3]
    **[1 mark for £1.65 × 4 = £6.60; 1 mark for £12.30 −
    £'6.60' = £'5.70'; 1 mark for £'5.70' ÷ 3 = £1.90]**
6. 53 [2]
    [1 mark for 4^3 = 64 or $\sqrt{121}$ = 11]
7. a) 23, 30 [1]
    b) $7n − 5$ [2]
        [1 mark for $7n$]
8. 29.5 [3]
    **[1 mark for (1 × 5) + (3 × 15) + (4 × 25) + (10 × 35) +
    (2 × 45) or 5 + 45 + 100 + 350 + 90 or 590; 1 mark for
    590 ÷ 20]**
9. $\begin{pmatrix} -12 \\ 8 \end{pmatrix}$ [2]
    [1 mark for −12 or 8]
10. 4 cm [2]
    **[1 mark for finding scale factor of 3, or for a ratio
    using two corresponding sides from same triangle or
    from similar triangles]**
11. $26.5\,cm^3$ [2]
    [1 mark for 135.13 ÷ 5.1]
12. Angle A = 45 degrees   Angle B = 90 degrees
    Angle C = 45 degrees
    Angle A = 36 degrees   Angle B = 72 degrees
    Angle C = 72 degrees [4]
    **[1 mark for 180 ÷ 4 (1 : 2 : 1) or 180 ÷ 5 (1 : 2 : 2);
    1 mark for 45 or 36; 1 mark for 45, 45, 90 or 36,
    72, 72]**
13. $1.5 × 10^3$ [2]
    [1 mark for 6 300 000 000 or 4 200 000 or 1500]
14. P(*B*) = 0.4 [3]
    **[1 mark for P(*B*) + P(*C*) = 1 − 0.35 = 0.65; 1 mark for
    2P(*B*) = 0.8]**

Pages 26–31: Calculate
Complete the example
Pythagoras' theorem says that $a^2 + b^2 = c^2$
Substituting in the numbers from the diagram gives
        $30^2 + 16^2 = AB^2$
This gives AB^2 = **1156** and so $AB = \sqrt{1156}$ = **34**
The length of *AB* is **34** cm
Exam practice questions
1. £7.92 [3]
    **[1 mark for 2.52 ÷ 3 or 0.84, or 96 ÷ 2 or 48; 1 mark
    for (2.52 ÷ 3 × 8) + (96 ÷ 2 × $2\frac{1}{2}$) or 6.72 + 1.20]**
2. a) 4.5 [1]
    b) −3.45 [2]
        [1 mark for (−30.15 + 6) ÷ 7 or −24.15 ÷ 7]
3. a) 438 [1]
    b) 7.3 [1]
4. a) 32.82 cm [1]
    b) $66.429\,cm^2$ [1]
5. 4.2 cm [2]
    [1 mark for 210 ÷ 50]

6. 99 degrees [2]
[1 mark for 360° − 73° − 89° or 198°]

7. a) 0.15 [3]
[1 mark for 1 − 0.25 − 0.15 or 0.4 or 0.6;
1 mark for 0.6 ÷ 4]
b) 36 [2]
[1 mark for 80 × 0.45]

8. £24 [5]
[1 mark for finding one part of the area of garden
36 or $\frac{9}{2}\pi$ or 14.137.... m²; 1 mark for 36 m² + $\frac{9}{2}\pi$ m²
or 50.137... m²; 1 mark for 50.137 ÷ 9 or 5.57.... or
6 bags; 1 mark for 6 × 4]

9. $\frac{24}{55}$ [3]
[1 mark for finding common multiple of 55 or 3 × 8 =
24; 1 mark for $\frac{3}{5} \times \frac{8}{11}$]

10. a) 79 507 [1]
b) 10 [1]

11. Jar B (the 500 g jar) [2]
[1 mark for $\frac{675}{300}$ or 2.25p per g or $\frac{1095}{500}$ or 2.19p per g
or $\frac{300}{675}$ or 0.44... g per pence or $\frac{500}{1095}$ or 0.456... g per
pence]

12. a) 459 [1]
b) 11 [1]
c) £44.10 [1]

Pages 32–35: Convert
Complete the example
1.5 km/minute = 1.5 × 60 km/h
        = 1.5 × 60 ÷ 1.6 mph
So 1.5 km/minute = **56.25** mph
Exam practice questions
1. a) 5% [1]
b) $\frac{1}{20}$ [2]
[1 mark for $\frac{5}{100}$]
2. 0.3125 [1]
3. 10 080 minutes [2]
[1 mark for 7 × 24 or 168 or 7 × 24 × 60 or 168 × 60]
4. 55 fl oz [2]
[1 mark for 1562 ÷ 28.4]
5. $438.60 [3]
[1 mark for 400 ÷ 1.14 or 350.877...; 1 mark for
'350.877...' × 1.25]
6. 16.7 m/s (1 d.p.) [2]
[1 mark for 60 × 1000 or 60 000 m or distance ÷ 60 ÷
60 or ÷ 3600 (seconds)]
7. 59°F [2]
[1 mark for 1.8 × 15 + 32]
8. a) 12.8 km [1]
b) 2.5 miles [accept 2.4 to 2.6 miles] [1]
c) 50 miles [1]
9. 3.5 [2]
[1 mark for 420 ÷ 120]

Pages 36–39: Simplify (fully)
Complete the example

Red : Blue : Orange	=	**16x** : **2x** : 4x
Red : Blue : Orange	=	**16** : **2** : 4
Red : Blue : Orange	=	**8** : **1** : **2**

Exam practice questions
1. a) 6d [1]
b) a − b [2]
[1 mark for each correct term]
c) −2cd [1]
d) −2x² [1]
2. a) 14a [1]
b) 18b² [1]
c) 28cd [1]
d) 12e⁵ [1]
3. 11 : 10 [2]
[1 mark for 275 : 250 or converting 25 cm into
250 mm]
4. a) 2^{11} [1]
b) 5^8 [1]
5. a) $16x^{12}$ [2]
[1 mark for 16 or x^{12}]
b) $4y^4$ [1]
6. (5x + 4) cm [2]
[1 mark for $\frac{6x + 4 + 5x - 17 + 4x + 25}{3}$ or $\frac{15x + 12}{3}$]
7. (9x − 3) cm [2]
[1 mark for x + 3 + 3x − 2 + 5x − 4 or 9x or − 3]
8. a) 4x² cm² [2]
[1 mark for 2x × 2x]
b) $(\pi y^2 - 4x^2)$ cm² [2]
[1 mark for area of circle = π × y × y or πy²;
1 mark for π × y × y − 4x² or πy² − 4x²]

Pages 40–43: Multiply out / Expand
Complete the example
(y + 3)(y + 5) means (y + 3) multiplied by (y + 5)
Multiplying each term inside the first bracket by each term
inside the second bracket:
y × y = **y²** and y × 5 = **5y**
3 × y = **3y** and 3 × **5** = **15**
Adding all the terms: **y² + 5y + 3y + 15**
Simplifying: **y² + 8y + 15**
Exam practice questions
1. a) 6x + 14 [1]
b) 8x − 9y [2]
[1 mark for −9y or 8x]
2. w³ + 5w [2]
[1 mark for w³ or 5w]
3. a) −8 + 6d [1]
b) 3a − 9 [1]
4. 8a − 7 [2]
[1 mark for 15a − 10 or −7a + 3]
5. a) p² − 6p + 9 [2]
[1 mark for p² − 3p − 3p + 9]

b) $4p^2 - 12p + 9$ **[2]**
[1 mark for $(4p^2 - 6p - 6p + 9)$, or three correct terms with correct signs, or four correct terms ignoring signs]

6. $2t^2 - 2t + 25$ **[3]**
[1 mark for $t^2 + 3t + 3t + 9$ or $t^2 - 4t - 4t + 16$;
1 mark for $t^2 + 6t + 9 + t^2 - 8t + 16$]

7. $(x + 2)(x + 5) = x^2 + 5x + 2x + 10 = (x^2 + 7x + 10)$ cm²   **[2]**
[1 mark for $(x + 2)(x + 5) = x^2 + 5x + 2x + 10$]

8. a) $x^2 + 3x - 10$ **[2]**
[1 mark for $(x^2 + 5x - 2x - 10)$, or three correct terms with correct signs, or four correct terms ignoring signs]

b) $10y^2 - 41y + 21$ **[2]**
[1 mark for $10y^2 - 35y - 6y + 21$]

9. $8x$ **[3]**
[1 mark for $x^2 + 2x + 2x + 4$ or $x^2 - 2x - 2x + 4$;
1 mark for $(x^2 + 4x + 4) - (x^2 - 4x + 4)$;
2 marks for using difference of two squares
$(x + 2 + x - 2)(x + 2 - (x - 2)) = 2x \times 4$]

Pages 44–47: Factorise (fully)
Complete the example
The two numbers in the brackets will multiply to equal 5 and add to equal 6:
$(x + 5)(x + 1)$

Exam practice questions
1. a) $3(a - 5)$ **[1]**
  b) $6(a + 4b)$ **[1]**
  c) $4(a + 2b + 3c)$ **[1]**
  d) $d(d + 1)$ **[1]**
  e) $7e(1 + 2e)$ **[1]**

2. a) $4c(4c - 1)$ **[2]**
[1 mark for $2c(8c - 2)$ or $c(16c - 4)$ or $4(4c^2 - 1)$]
  b) $5d(-2d^2 + 3d + 1)$ **[2]**
[1 mark for $5(-2d^3 + 3d^2 + d)$ or $d(-10d^2 + 15d + 5)$]

3. $4x(3x + 2)$ **[1]**

4. a) $2ef(2f + 3eg)$ **[2]**
[1 mark for $2e(2f^2 + 3efg)$ or $2f(2ef + 3e^2g)$ or $ef(4f + 6eg)$]
  b) $3xy(5x^2 - 2xy^2 + 7y)$ **[2]**
[1 mark for $3x(5x^2y - 2xy^3 + 7y^2)$
or $3y(5x^2 - 2x^2y^2 + 7xy)$ or $xy(15x^2 - 6xy^2 + 21y)$]

5. $(x - 3)(x - 4)$ **[1]**

6. a) $(x + 3)(x + 5)$ **[2]**
[1 mark for $(x + 3)$ or $(x + 5)$]
  b) $(x + 7)(x - 5)$ **[2]**
[1 mark for $(x \pm 7)(x \pm 5)$]
  c) $(x - 8)(x - 3)$ **[2]**
[1 mark for $(x \pm 8)(x \pm 3)$]
  d) $(x + 2)(x - 9)$ **[2]**
[1 mark for $(x \pm 2)(x \pm 9)$]

7. a) $(x + 3)(x - 3)$ **[1]**
  b) $(x + 11)(x - 11)$ **[1]**

Pages 48–51: Solve / Rearrange
Complete the example
Subtracting the equations to eliminate a:
$$a + 3b = 17$$
$$\underline{a + b = 7}$$
$$2b = 10$$
And solving to find b: $b = 5$

Substituting $b = 5$ into one of the original equations:
$$a + (3 \times 5) = 17$$
$$a + 15 = 17$$
$$a = 2$$
Finally, checking the answers by substituting into the other equation:
$$2 + 5 = 7$$

Exam practice questions
1. a) $a = 21$ **[1]**
  b) $b = 48$ **[1]**
  c) $c = \frac{1}{8}$ or 0.125 **[1]**

2. $x = \frac{y + 6}{3}$ or $x = \frac{y}{3} + 2$ **[2]**
[1 mark for $3x = y + 6$ or $x - 2 = \frac{y}{3}$]

3. a) $a = 7$ **[2]**
[1 mark for $8a = 66 - 10$ or $8a = 56$]
  b) $b = 8$ **[2]**
[1 mark for $6b - 2b = 20 + 12$ or $4b = 32$]
  c) $c = -\frac{1}{2}$ **[2]**
[1 mark for $3c - 3 = 7c - 1$ or $7c - 3c = -3 + 1$ or $4c = -2$]

4. $x = 22.5$ degrees   **[3]**
[1 mark for $6x - 35 + 3x - 22 + x + 12$ or $10x - 45$;
1 mark for $10x - 45 = 180$]

5. $x = 3y + 4$ **[2]**
[1 mark for $3y = x - 4$]

6. $x = 3.5, y = -0.5$ **[3]**
[1 mark for elimination of one variable $x + 3x = 3 + 11$
or $4x = 14$ or $3y + y = 9 - 11$ or $4y = -2$;
1 mark for $x = 3.5$ or $y = -0.5$]

7. $x < 7$ **[2]**
[1 mark for or $3x < 21$]

8. $x = -4$ or $x = 3$ **[3]**
[1 mark for $(x \pm a)(x \pm b)$ where $ab = -12$;
1 mark for $(x + 4)(x - 3)$]

9. $x = 2, y = 7$ **[1]**

Pages 52–55: Match

Complete the example

A regular hexagon has 6 sides so

Step 1   Exterior angle = 360° ÷ 6 = **60°**

Step 2   Interior angle = 180° − **60°** = **120°**

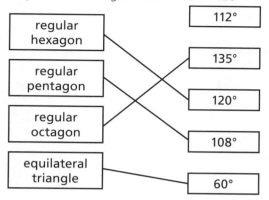

Exam practice questions

1.

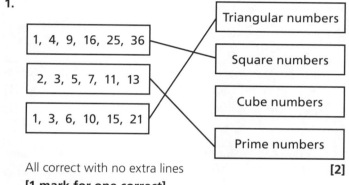

All correct with no extra lines [2]

[1 mark for one correct]

2.

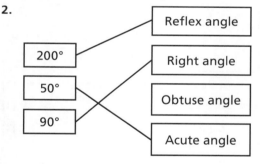

All correct with no extra lines [2]

[1 mark for one correct]

3.

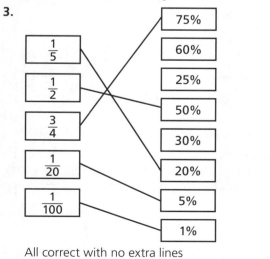

All correct with no extra lines [4]

[3 marks for three correct; 2 marks for two correct; 1 mark for one correct]

4.

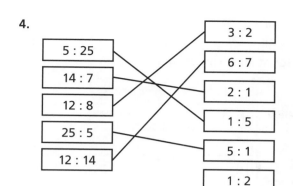

All correct with no extra lines [3]

[2 marks for two or three correct; 1 mark for one correct]

5.

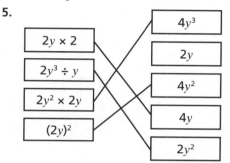

All correct with no extra lines [3]

[2 marks for two correct; 1 mark for one correct]

6.

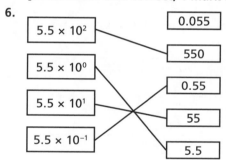

All correct with no extra lines [3]

[2 marks for two correct; 1 mark for one correct]

7.

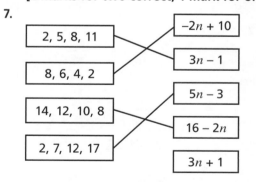

All correct with no extra lines [3]

[2 marks for two correct; 1 mark for one correct]

Pages 56–59: Complete / List

Complete the example

Writing down all the two-digit numbers starting with 1.

14, 18, 19

Then all the two-digit numbers starting with 4.

And so on.

14, 18, 19, 41, **48**, **49**, 81, **84**, **89**, 91, **94**, **98**

Exam practice questions

1. BB, BW, BR, BP, WW, WR, WP, RR, RP, PP   **[2]**
   [1 mark for at least six correct]

2.

Drink	Tally	Frequency
Tea	IIII I	6
Coffee	IIII	5
Juice	IIII	4
		Total = 15

   All correct   **[2]**
   [1 mark for all three tallies correct]

3.

First dice

Second dice		1	2	3	4	5	6
	1	2	3	4	5	6	7
	2	3	4	5	6	7	8
	3	4	5	6	7	8	9
	4	5	6	7	8	9	10
	5	6	7	8	9	10	11
	6	7	8	9	10	11	12

   All correct   **[2]**
   [1 mark for at least 10 correct values]

4. 1, 2, 4, 8, 16, 32   **[2]**
   [1 mark for four or five correct values with no incorrect values]

5.

	Won	Drawn	Lost	Total
Home	**19**	**3**	1	23
Away	**7**	11	**2**	**20**
Total	26	**14**	3	43

   All correct   **[3]**
   [1 mark for three correct values; 2 marks for five correct values]

6. 3, 4, 5, 6, 7, 8, 9   **[2]**
   [1 mark for 2.5 or $\frac{5}{2}$]

7.

Colour of bead	Number of beads
Grey	n
Black	$n + 4$
Orange	$2(n + 4)$ or $2n + 8$
Purple	$2(n + 4) - 3$ or $2n + 5$

       [3]

   [1 mark for each correct row]

8.

	Women	Men	Total
Left-handed	6	15	21
Right-handed	14	45	59
Total	20	60	80

       [5]

   [1 mark for total men = 60; 1 mark for 15 left-handed men; 1 mark for 45 right-handed men; 1 mark for 6 left-handed women or 14 right-handed women]

Pages 60–63: Estimate

Complete the example

Use a ruler to draw a line from $y = 5$ to intersect with the curve.

Use a ruler to draw lines from the intersection of $y = 5$ and the curve to the **x-axis**.

When $y = 5$, $x \approx 2.6$ and $x \approx 5.4$

Exam practice questions

1. 8.1 rounds to 10, 45.8 rounds to 50, 18 rounds to 20   **[1]**
   $\frac{10 \times 50}{20} = \frac{500}{20} = 25$ **[1]**

2. $\frac{38}{200} = \frac{19}{100}$ **[1]**

3.

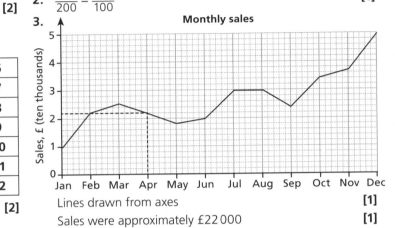

Monthly sales

   Lines drawn from axes   **[1]**
   Sales were approximately £22 000   **[1]**

4.

Time (t minutes)	Frequency (f)	Midpoint	Midpoint × f
$0 < t \leqslant 10$	15	**5**	**$5 \times 15 = 75$**
$10 < t \leqslant 20$	25	**15**	**$15 \times 25 = 375$**
$20 < t \leqslant 30$	10	**25**	**$25 \times 10 = 250$**
$30 < t \leqslant 40$	5	**35**	**$35 \times 5 = 175$**

   Multiplying at least three midpoints × f correctly   **[1]**
   Mean = $\frac{75 + 375 + 250 + 175}{15 + 25 + 10 + 5}$ **[1]**
   = 15.91 minutes (2 d.p.)   **[1]**

5.

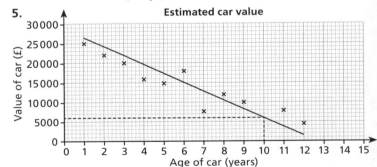

Estimated car value

   Line of best fit   **[1]**
   Lines drawn on graph from $x = 10$ to the line of best fit and to the y-axis   **[1]**
   e.g. £6000   **[accept an accurate answer (within £500) from the line of best fit drawn]**   **[1]**

6.

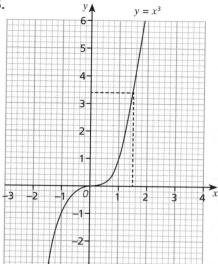

Lines drawn on graph from axes [1]

$1.5^3 \approx 3.4$ [1]

[Accept any answer from 3.35 to 3.45 inclusive]

Pages 64–69: Draw / Sketch / Plot
Complete the example

Chemistry: $\frac{1}{4}$ of **360°** = **90°**

Biology: 40% of 360° = (360 ÷ 10) × **4** = **144°**

Physics: 360° – (**90° + 144°**) = **126°**

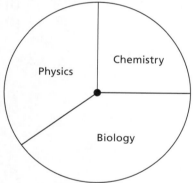

1. a) *Any suitable answer, e.g.* [1]

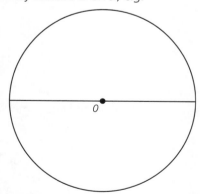

[The diameter can be drawn in any direction but it must pass through the centre of the circle and touch the circumference at each end]

b) *Any suitable answer, e.g.* [1]

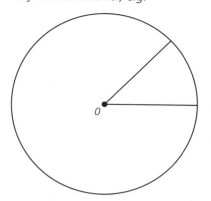

[The sector can be drawn in any part of the circle but must consist of two radii]

2.

Butterflies seen

The chart should have:
- Scale starting at 0 and increasing by 1
- *y*-axis labelled as Frequency, *f* or Number
- *x*-axis labelled with butterfly types
- A suitable title given (e.g. Butterflies seen)
- Bars labelled with the names of the butterflies
- Bars of equal widths
- Equal gaps between each bar
- All heights correct

All correct [3]

[2 marks for at least five features correct; 1 mark for at least three features correct]

3. Rectangle with a length of 8 cm and a width of 5 cm [1]

4.

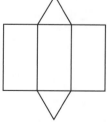

[2]

[1 mark for at least three faces drawn]

5.

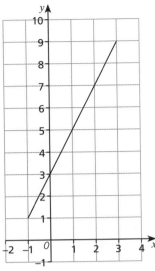

Correct calculation of at least two points: (−1, 1), (0, 3), [1]
(1, 5), (2, 7), (3, 9)
At least two points plotted correctly on the grid [1]
Straight line drawn through the points [1]

6.

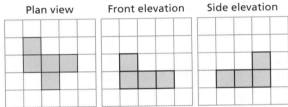

Plan view   Front elevation   Side elevation

[1 mark for each] [3]

7. 34 or 35 [2]

[Reading depends on line of best fit drawn;
1 mark for a suitable line of best fit drawn]

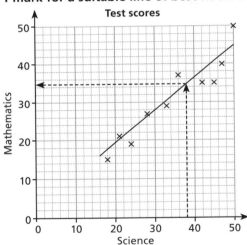

8. General shape of parabola [1]
y-intercept (0, 3) labelled [1]

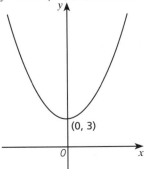

(0, 3)

Pages 70–73: Is … correct?

Complete the example

2.9 rounded to the nearest integer is **3**

5.7 rounded to the nearest integer is **6**

9.5 rounded to the nearest integer is **10**

Estimate for the area of the base is **3** cm × **6** cm = **18** cm²

Substituting the estimated values in the formula,

$$V = \frac{1}{3} \times \mathbf{18} \times \mathbf{10} = \mathbf{60}\,\text{cm}^3$$

Each dimension has been rounded up to the nearest integer, so 60 cm³ is an **overestimate**.

The volume cannot be **greater** than 60 cm³, so he is **incorrect**.

Exam practice questions

1. No. $\frac{23}{5} = 4\frac{3}{5}$ [1]

2. Yes and correct method.

24 ÷ 3 × 2 or 16 [1]

16 × 60 or 960 [1]

3. No and correct reason, e.g.

The bar for vanilla is higher than 30 [1]

4. No. 11 is not a multiple of 2 so you cannot fill up all the space in the box. [1]

5. No. The correct error interval is

1.55 m ⩽ length < 1.65 m [2]

[1 mark for one correct value]

6. No. $(a + 2)(a − 1) = a^2 − a + 2a − 2$ [1]

$= a^2 + a − 2$ [1]

Pages 74–79: Use (a given method)

Complete the example

$\sin x = \dfrac{6}{12}$

$x = \sin^{-1}\left(\dfrac{1}{2}\right)$

$x = \mathbf{30}$ degrees

Exam practice questions

1. a) 23 × 5 or 25 × 3 [1]

    b) 32 × 5 or 35 × 2 [1]

    c) $\dfrac{2 + 2}{3 + 5}$ [1]

2. a) 201 [1]

    b) (2000 + 30) ÷ 10 [1]

       = 203 [1]

       Yes, the answer is sensible. [1]

3. Mast on page measured to be 4 cm and house measured to be 1 cm [1]

    7.5 × 4 = 30 m [1]

4. Distance is 6 × 200 000 = 1 200 000 cm

    = 1 200 000 ÷ 100 or 12 000 m

    = 12 000 ÷ 1000 = 12 km [3]

[2 marks for × 200 000, ÷ 100 and ÷ 1000;
1 mark for any two calculations]

5. a) 125 [1]

    b) Dance [1]

    c) Swimming and football [1]

6. a)

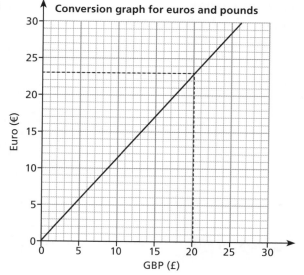

Conversion graph for euros and pounds

€23   **[1]**

b)

Pounds (£)	Euros (€)
10	**11.50**
20	**23**
40	**46**

[2]

[1 mark for two correct]

7. $35^2 + 12^2 = x^2$ **[1]**

     $\sqrt{35^2 + 12^2}$ **[1]**

     $= 37$ cm   **[1]**

8. a) $5 + 10 + 7 + 3 = 25$ **[1]**

    b)   3   **[1]**

    c)   5   **[1]**

9. a) $x = -3$ and $x = 1$ **[1]**

    b) $(-1, -4)$ **[1]**

    c) $(0, -3)$ **[1]**

10. 720 degrees   **[2]**

    [1 mark for 4 × 180]

Pages 80–83: Translate / Reflect / Rotate / Enlarge

Complete the example

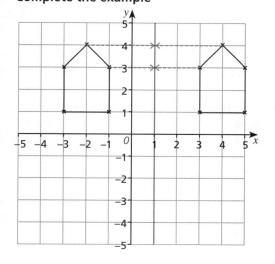

1. *Enlarged triangle can be placed anywhere on the grid:*

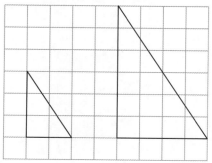

[2]

[1 mark if points are not connected]

2.

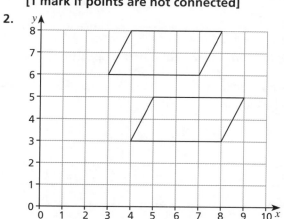

[2]

[1 mark for an answer moved 1 left or 3 up]

3.

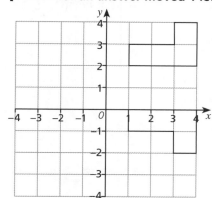

[2]

[1 mark for a reflection in the line $x = 1$]

4.

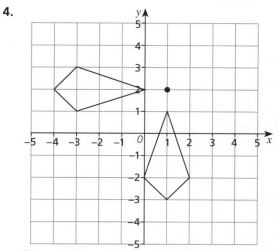

[2]

[1 mark for a rotation 90° anticlockwise or for a rotation 90° clockwise around the wrong point]

5.

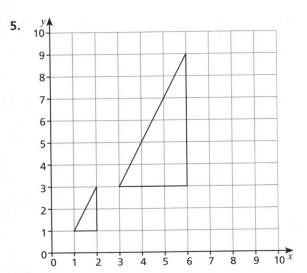

[2]

[1 mark for correct size but incorrect position]

Pages 84–87: Describe

Complete the example

$$-2 \quad 1 \quad 4 \quad 7 \quad 10$$

$$+3 \quad +3 \quad +3 \quad +3$$

Position	1	2	3	4	5	n
Term	–2	1	4	7	10	?
Times table	1×3 $= 3$	2×3 $= 6$	3×3 $= 9$	4×3 $= 12$	5×3 $= 15$	$n \times 3$ $= 3n$
Difference between the term and the times table	$-2 - 3$ $= -5$	$1 - 6$ $= -5$	$4 - 9$ $= -5$	$7 - 12$ $= -5$	$10 - 15$ $= -5$	$3n - 5$

The nth term rule is $3n - 5$

Exam practice questions

1. negative; positive [1]
2. Reflection [1]
   in the line $y = -1$ [1]
3. Add two previous terms to obtain the next term
   (Fibonacci) [1]
4. Rotation [1]
   90° anticlockwise [1]
   about the point (–1, 1) [1]
5. Positive (or strong positive) correlation [1]
6. Enlargement [1]
   with a scale factor of 2 [1]
   from the point (4, 9) [1]

Pages 88–91: Construct

Complete the example

1. Put the point of the compasses on the vertex of **the angle** and draw an arc intersecting **BA** and **BC**.
2. Put the point of the compasses on the intersection of the arc and **the line BA** (or **BC**). Draw an arc in the middle of the angle.
3. Keep the compasses the same distance apart. Repeat step 2 on the other intersection.
4. Line up the ruler and draw a line from the **vertex** of the angle to the intersecting arcs from steps 2 and 3.

Exam practice questions

1.

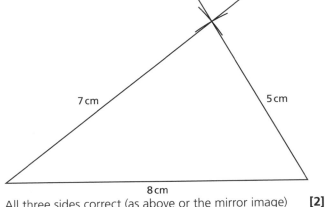

All three sides correct (as above or the mirror image) **[2]**

[1 mark for arcs drawn but sides not joined]

2.

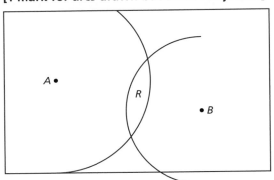

Arc with radius 5 cm, centre A [1]
Arc with radius 4 cm, centre B [1]
Intersecting region marked R (allow shading if clear) [1]

3.

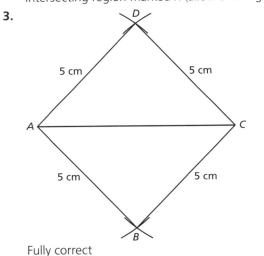

Fully correct [3]

[2 marks for two pairs of 5 cm arcs from A and C intersecting with no lines drawn; 1 mark for one arc from A and one arc from C intersecting]

4.

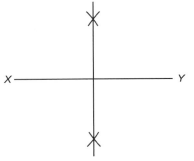

Fully correct with perpendicular bisector drawn **[2]**

[1 mark for intersecting arcs of equal radii drawn from points X and Y]

5.

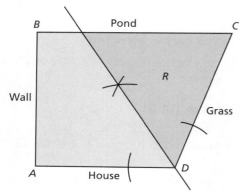

Arcs from *D* of equal radii drawn on line *AD* and line *DC*. [1]

Intersecting arcs drawn from the point of intersection of the arcs and the lines on both *AD* and *DC*. [1]

Correct angle bisector drawn. [1]

Pages 92–97: Give your answer

Complete the example

Area of the circle is $\pi \times 5^2 = 25\pi$ cm^2

Area of the square is $10 \times 10 = 100$ cm^2

Shaded area = ($100 - 25\pi$) cm^2

Exam practice questions

1. $\dfrac{15}{8}$ [1]

   $= 1\dfrac{7}{8}$ [1]

2. (South is) 180° [1]

3. 3000 [2]

   [1 mark for 12000 × 250 or for ÷ 1000]

4. $\dfrac{2}{100}$ or 2 out of 100 [1]

   0.02 [1]

5. £21.61 [2]

   [1 mark for £540.30 ÷ 25 or 21.612]

6. 63.6 cm^2 [2]

   [1 mark for $\pi \times 4.5^2$ or 63.61…]

7. 46 × 30 + 34 × 231 [1]

   = 9234 [1]

   £92.34 [1]

8. Arc length for Y $= \dfrac{3}{8} \times 2 \times \pi \times 8$ or 6π [3]

   [1 mark for 2 × π × 8; 1 mark for $\dfrac{3}{8}$]

   Perimeter = (6π + 16) cm [1]

9. 75 mph [2]

   [1 mark for 0.25 × 5 × 60 or 1.25 miles in a minute]

10. 25.90 [2]

    [1 mark for 25.903…]

11. $3x^2$ cm^2 [2]

    [1 mark for $\dfrac{1}{2} \times 3x \times 2x$]

12. a) 10 × 40 = 400 cm^2 [2]

    [1 mark for 0.1 m = 10 cm and 0.4 m = 40 cm]

    b) 20000 cm^3 [2]

    [1 mark for 10 × 40 × 50]

Pages 98–101: Give a reason / an example

Complete the example

The error interval for the roll is **9.5** m ⩽ length < **10.5** m

The total length of the four pieces is 4 × 2.6 = **10.4** m

This is within the error interval so he could be correct.

Exam practice questions

1. No, his method is incorrect, He should have done

   (8 ÷ 2) + (3 × 4) = 4 + 12 = 16 [2]

   [1 mark for (8 ÷ 2) + (3 × 4) or 4 + 12]

2. a) Yes. Triangular numbers are 1, 3, 6, 10 … or 1, 1 + 2, 1 + 2 + 3, 1 + 2 + 3 + 4 … which follows the same sequence. [1]

   b) 4950. Number of white triangles in a pattern is always the same as the number of black triangles in the previous pattern. [1]

3. P(A) = 0.7

   P(B) = 1 − 0.2 or 0.5 + 0.3 = 0.8

   P(C) = 0.3 + 0.3 = 0.6, so B is most likely. [2]

   [1 mark for any two correct probabilities]

4. 37° + 92° + 51° = 180° [1]

5. Sides are 7 cm, 7 cm and 2 cm so isosceles [2]

   [1 mark for at least two correct lengths]

6. An ordinary coin has an equally likely chance of landing on heads or tails so could land on heads. [1]

7. Median is middle value so between 25th and 26th height.

   Median must be in the class 1.4 ⩽ h < 1.6

   so cannot be 1.6 [1]

8. a) Jug B as the graph is a straight line [2]

   b) Jug A as the graph reaches 20 cm first (after approx. 4.4 seconds) [2]

9. SAS (side, angle, side) [1]

Pages 102–105: Criticise / Identify any mistakes / What error?

Complete the example

1. The vertical scale should start at **0**.

2. The vertical scale also needs a **label** (e.g. **frequency**).

Exam practice questions

1. Mistakes are − 2 should be + 2, and − 7 − 2 should be −9 [2]

   [1 mark for identifying each error]

   Alternative mark scheme:

   Correct working is $8x - 7 - (3x - 2) = 8x - 7 - 3x + 2$

   $= 5x - 5$ [2]

   [1 mark for each line]

2. It has **one** line of symmetry [1]

   One pair of opposite angles are equal [1]

3. a) It should be £1.95 ÷ 1000 (as 1 kg = 1000 grams) [1]

   b) It should be 1000 ÷ 195 (as working in pence) [1]

4. He has increased £300 by 20% as 1.2 is the multiplier for increasing by 20%. [1]

5. There should be semi-circular arcs at each end. [1]

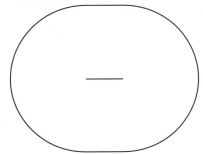

6. The working should be:

$x^2 + 4^2 = 9^2$ or $x^2 = 9^2 - 4^2$ [1]

$x^2 + 16 = 81$ or $x^2 = 81 - 16$ [1]

$x^2 = 65$

$x = \sqrt{65}$, $x = 8.1\,\text{cm}$ (1 d.p.) [1]

[1 mark each can be awarded for identifying that errors are in adding on line 1 and incorrect squaring on line 2]

Pages 106–109: Compare

Complete the example

50% of £50 $= \frac{1}{2} \times £50 = $ **£25**

$\frac{3}{5}$ of £40 $= \frac{3}{5} \times £40 = $ **£24**

$0.7 \times £30 = $ **£21**

So in order of value starting from the smallest.

$0.7 \times £30$, $\frac{3}{5}$ of £40, 50% of £50

Exam practice questions

1. a) Area of rectangle $= 3 \times 8 = 24\,\text{cm}^2$

Area of square $= 5.5 \times 5.5 = 30.25\,\text{cm}^2$

So square has the greater area. [2]

[1 mark for a correct area]

b) Perimeter of rectangle $= 2(3 + 8) = 22\,\text{cm}$

Perimeter of square $= 4 \times 5.5 = 22\,\text{cm}$

So both have same perimeter. [2]

[1 mark for a correct perimeter]

2. Percentage of boys $= 52\%$, percentage of girls $= 48\%$

So greater percentage of boys [1]

Average age of girls is greater [1]

Numbers with special needs:

Boys $= 58$, Girls $= 64$ so more girls [1]

3.

Amount, A (£)	Midpoint	Frequency	Midpoint × frequency
$0 \leqslant A < 10$	5	23	115
$10 \leqslant A < 20$	15	14	210
$20 \leqslant A < 30$	25	3	75
			Total = 400

Estimated mean amount for the 40 people =

$(115 + 210 + 75) \div 40 = £10$

Greater for these 40 than for the average

British worker. [4]

[1 mark for 115, 210 and 75 or 400; 1 mark for £10; 1 mark for correct division]

4. Pressure on object A $= \frac{120}{0.5} = 240\,\text{N/m}^2$ [1]

Pressure on object B $= \frac{180}{1.5} = 120\,\text{N/m}^2$ [1]

Pressure greater on object A or Pressure double on object

A compared to object B [1]

Pages 110–113: Show (that)

Complete the example

Listing the square numbers up to 100 gives 1, 4, 9, **16**, **25**, 36, **49**, **64**, **81**, 100

Listing the numbers that are 1 more than the square numbers gives 2, 5, 10, **17**, **26**, **37**, **50**, **65**, **82**, 101

The prime numbers less than 100 in this list are 2, 5, **17** and **37**.

There are four prime numbers less than 100 in the list.

Exam practice questions

1. 1 and 6, 2 and 5, 3 and 4, 4 and 3, 5 and 2, 6 and 1 [2]

[1 mark for at least three ways shown]

2. Exterior angle $= 180° - 120° = 60°$ [1]

Number of sides $= 360° \div 60° = 6$, so hexagon [1]

3. *Decimal method:*

Fractions are 0.75   0.625, 0.65, 0.66... or 0.67, 0.8

Closest value is 0.8 or $\frac{4}{5}$ [2]

[1 mark for at least three out of five correct conversions]

Fraction method:

e.g. using 40 as common denominator

$\frac{3}{4} = \frac{30}{40}$ $\frac{5}{8} = \frac{25}{40}$ $\frac{13}{20} = \frac{26}{40}$ $\frac{2}{3} = \frac{26.6...}{40}$ $\frac{4}{5} = \frac{32}{40}$

Closest value is $\frac{4}{5}$ [2]

[1 mark for at least three out of five fractions with a common denominator]

4.

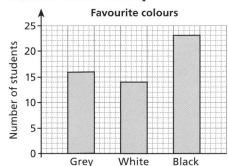

Fully correct bar chart [3]

[1 mark for title and vertical axis label; 1 mark for bars with correct heights 16, 14 and 23]

5. a) $C = \pi \times \text{diameter} = \pi \times 60 = 188.49...$ [1]

$= 190$ (to nearest 10 centimetres) [1]

b) $1\,\text{km} = 1000\,\text{m} = 100\,000\,\text{cm}$ [1]

Number of rotations $= 100\,000 \div 188.49$ [1]

$= 530.53$ so more than 500 [1]

6. Testing $h = 5\,\text{cm}$

Volume of prism $=$ area of cross-section $\times$ length

$= \frac{1}{2} \times 6 \times 5 \times 10$ [1]

$= 150\,\text{cm}^3$ [1]

Alternative method:

Volume of prism $=$ area of cross-section $\times$ length,

so $\frac{1}{2}$ × 6 × h × 10 = 150 **[1]**

$h = \frac{150 \times 2}{6 \times 10} = 5$ cm **[1]**

7. 52 ÷ 13 = 4 **[1]**

8 × 4 = 32 and 5 × 4 = 20 **[1]**

32 − 20 = 12 **[1]**

Alternative method:

52 ÷ 13 = 4 **[1]**

8 − 5 = 3 **[1]**

3 × 4 = 12 **[1]**

8. Gradient of $y = 7 - 3x$ is − 3 **[1]**

$6x + 2y = 6$ rearranges to $y = -3x + 3$,

so gradient is also −3 **[1]**

Same gradients so the lines are parallel **[1]**

9. Mode = 10

Putting numbers in order gives 9, 10, 10, 15, 16, 18, so median = 12.5

Mean = (9 + 10 + 10 + 15 + 16 + 18) ÷ 6 or 78 ÷ 6 = 13

So, mode < median < mean **[3]**

[1 mark for one average correct; 2 marks for two averages correct]

10. Possibilities are 20 × 1, 10 × 2, 5 × 4 **[1]**

Perimeters of these are 20 + 1 + 20 + 1 = 42 cm

10 + 2 + 10 + 2 = 24 cm, 5 + 4 + 5 + 4 = 18 cm **[1]**

So 1 possibility out of 3, therefore probability = $\frac{1}{3}$ **[1]**

Pages 114–119: Mixed questions

1. a)

Millimetres (mm)	Centimetres (cm)	Metres (m)	Kilometres (km)
9000	**900**	9	**0.009**
60	6	**0.06**	0.00006

[2]

[1 mark for each correct row]

b) No and correct method

6 cm = 0.06 m **or** 9 m = 900 cm

6 cm + 900 cm = 906 cm = 9.06 m **or** 0.06 m + 9 m = 9.06 m **[1]**

2. a)

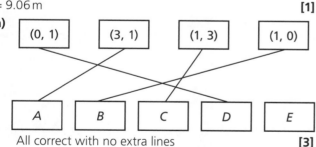

All correct with no extra lines **[3]**

[1 mark for each box correctly matched]

b) *Any two from: ABDC, ADBE, AEBC* **[2]**

[1 mark for one correct]

3. a) (0, −3) **[1]**

b) 3 **[1]**

c) $2y - 6x = 8$ **[1]**

4. a) *Valid method of comparison (e.g. common denominator, changing to decimals, subtracting fractions)*

Example method 1:

e.g. $\frac{5}{9} = \frac{70}{126}, \frac{1}{2} = \frac{63}{126}, \frac{4}{7} = \frac{72}{126}$ **[2]**

[1 mark for comparing any two fractions]

Example method 2:

e.g. $\frac{5}{9} = 0.555..., \frac{1}{2} = 0.5, \frac{4}{7} = 0.571...$ **[2]**

[1 mark for comparing any two decimals]

Example method 3:

e.g. $\frac{5}{9} - \frac{1}{2} = 0.555... - 0.5 = 0.055...$

So $\frac{5}{9}$ is greater than $\frac{1}{2}$ and $\frac{4}{7} - \frac{5}{9} = 0.015...$

So $\frac{5}{9}$ is less than $\frac{4}{7}$ **[2]**

[1 mark for one comparison]

b) $1\frac{4}{5}$ **[2]**

[1 mark for $\frac{9}{5}$]

5. a) Perimeter of triangle : Perimeter of square is 18 : 20 **[1]**

= 9 : 10 **[1]**

b) New perimeter of square = 20 cm × 0.9 **[1]**

= 18 cm **[1]**

So new ratio is 18 : 18 = 1 : 1 **[1]**

6. a) $\frac{7}{9}$ **[1]**

b) Area of room is 4.7 × 3 × 4 = 56.4 m² **[1]**

Area to be painted is 4.7 × 3 × 4 × 2 or

56.4 × 2 = 112.8 m² **[1]**

Paint required = 112.8 ÷ 13 = 8.67... litres **[1]**

= 9 litres to nearest litre **[1]**

7. a) 2 × 2 × 3 × 3 × 5 or 2² × 3² × 5 **[2]**

[1 mark for at least two different factors seen, 2 and 5 or 2 and 3 or 3 and 5]

b) 2² × 3 × 5 **[1]**

8. a) (4.3 + 7.1) × 101 = 11.4 × 101 **[1]**

= 11.4 × 100 + 11.4 × 1 = 1140 + 11.4 = 1151.4 **[1]**

b) (4 + 7) × 100 = 1100 so sensible **[2]**

[1 mark for 4, 7 and 100]

9. a) Conclusion justified by reference to closeness to 20, e.g. No and should all be close to 20 **or** Yes and as all are fairly close to 20 **[1]**

b) $\frac{15}{100}$ or $\frac{3}{20}$ or 0.15 **[1]**

10. a) $2x + 3 = 39$ **[1]**

[can be any letter for x]

b) $2x = 39 - 3$ or $2x = 36$ **[1]**

18 or $x = 18$ **[1]**

11. a) $5 \leqslant t < 10$ **[1]**

b) Choose a minimum value from $0 \leqslant t < 5$ and a maximum value from $20 \leqslant t < 25$ with a difference of 23. **[1]**

Shows that maximum − minimum = 23, e.g. 24 − 1 = 23 **[1]**

12. a) Amount = £3000 × 1.04²

= £3244.80 **[2]**

[1 mark for 1.04²]

b) It earns less interest, equivalent to £3000 simple interest for 2 years.

Or £6000 earns £240 compared with £244.80 for part a) **[1]**

13. a) All 10 points plotted correctly **[3]**

[2 marks for at least seven points plotted correctly; 1 mark for at least four points plotted correctly]

b) Line of best fit drawn **[1]**

c) Correct reading for line of best fit, e.g. 20 minutes **[1]**

14. a) $(x + 4)(x - 9)$ **[2]**

[1 mark for $(x + a)(x + b)$ where $ab = -36$ or $a + b = -5$]

b) $x = -4$ or $x = 9$ **[1]**

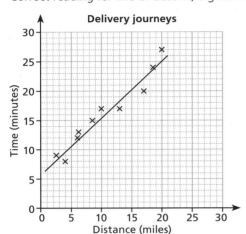

Delivery journeys — graph of Time (minutes) against Distance (miles)

Acknowledgements

The authors and publisher are grateful to the copyright holders for permission to use quoted materials and images.
Every effort has been made to trace copyright holders and obtain their permission for the use of copyright material. The authors and publisher will gladly receive information enabling them to rectify any error or omission in subsequent editions. All facts are correct at time of going to press.
All images ©Shutterstock and HarperCollins*Publishers*

Published by Collins

An imprint of HarperCollins*Publishers* Limited
1 London Bridge Street
London SE1 9GF

HarperCollins*Publishers*
Macken House
39/40 Mayor Street Upper
Dublin 1
D01 C9W8
Ireland

British Library Cataloguing in Publication Data.

A CIP record of this book is available from the British Library.
Publisher: Katie Sergeant
Authors: Trevor Senior, Anne Stothers and Leisa Bovey
Commissioning and Project Management: Richard Toms
Inside Concept Design: Ian Wrigley and Sarah Duxbury
Layout: Ian Wrigley and Contentra Technologies
Cover Design: Sarah Duxbury
Production: Bethany Brohm
Printed in the United Kingdom by Martins the Printers

MIX
Paper | Supporting responsible forestry
FSC™ C007454

This book contains FSC™ certified paper and other controlled sources to ensure responsible forest management.

For more information visit: www.harpercollins.co.uk/green